C000007592

Call of
the Wild

A celebration of British landscapes
edited by Roly Smith

Call of the Wild

Published 2005 by Rucksack Readers, Landrick Lodge,
Dunblane, FK15 0HY, UK

Telephone	0/+44 1786 824 696
Website	**www.rucsacs.com**
Email	info@rucsacs.com

Distributed in North America by Interlink Publishing, 46 Crosby Street,
Northampton, Mass, 01060, USA (**www.interlinkbooks.com**)

© design and layout copyright Rucksack Readers 2005; text and
photographs © copyright 2005 the contributors as identified on pages
5 and 126

All rights reserved. No part of this publication may be reproduced,
stored in a retrieval system, or transmitted in any form or by any
means, electronic, mechanical, photocopying, recording or otherwise,
without prior permission in writing from the publisher and copyright
holders.

ISBN 1-898481-49-0

British Library cataloguing in publication data: a catalogue record for
this book is available from the British Library.

Designed in Scotland by WorkHorse (info@workhorse.co.uk)

Colour separation by HK Scanner Arts International Ltd, Hong Kong

Printed in China by Hong Kong Graphics & Printing Ltd

Front cover: Sunset on Taransay
Title page: Hengwm Valley
Back cover: Walker crossing moorland between
Higher Shelf Stones and Bleaklow Head

Call of the Wild

A celebration of British landscapes
edited by Roly Smith

In affectionate memory of
Derryck Draper (1933-2004), founder member and
former chairman of the Outdoor Writers' Guild

Call of the Wild

Contents

Foreword

Playing the wild card

Wilderness is a difficult concept to pin down. To some people, it may be a virgin landscape untouched by Man, like the higher Himalaya, the ice-bound Arctic or Antarctic wastes, or the arid deserts of Asia, Africa or America.

As someone who has been lucky enough to spend time in all these places, I can vouch for the ultimate wilderness experiences they provide. But I can honestly say that I've had equal, if not greater, wilderness experiences in the British Isles. To give just one example, not so long ago I found myself seriously lost among the peat hags and groughs of Kinder Scout, a mere 10 miles from the centres of Manchester and Sheffield.

My own local 'wilderness' is the open fells and secret valleys 'Back o' Skiddaw' near my home in the northern Lakes. This is where I go regularly to escape the stresses and strains of a hectic world, and here I find I can lose and recreate myself – mentally and physically – just as easily as in a remote, untrodden Himalayan valley.

The essays in this book – all written, edited and illustrated by fellow members of the Outdoor Writers' Guild to mark the Guild's 25th anniversary – clearly show that this essential wild country can still be found on our doorsteps in most areas of the British Isles.

Perhaps you have already found your own treasured wilderness. If not, I hope these personal essays, photographs and illustrations from members of the OWG will inspire you to go out and find it.

As Henry David Thoreau, a man who found his personal wilderness in a tiny log cabin in the woods of Walden Pond in Massachusetts, first said in his 1862 essay on Walking: '…in Wildness is the preservation of the World'.

ilda, the Lovers' Stone

Chris Bonington

Introduction

Roly Smith
Born to be wild

It may seem strange, in a crowded and heavily-industrialised country such as Britain, to talk about the 'call of the wild'. But as Chris Bonington points out in his Foreword, wilderness is a relative term, and a sense of wildness can still be experienced by those like Thoreau who are prepared to go out and look for it, in almost any corner of these beautiful and infinitely varied islands.

And it is essential that we do. As John Muir, the Scots-born father of National Parks, once said: 'Everybody needs beauty as well as bread, places to play in and pray in, where Nature may heal and cheer and give strength to body and soul.'

In the introduction to his 1901 book *Our National Parks* he famously added: 'Thousands of tired, nerve-shaken, over-civilised people are beginning to find out that going to the mountains is going home; that wildness is a necessity; and that mountain parks and reservations are useful not only as fountains of timber and irrigating rivers, but as fountains of life.'

If, as Muir so perceptively suggested, wildness was a necessary antidote to the pressures of modern living over a century ago, surely we need it even more in today's hectic world of instant, electronic global communication and commerce.

One thing is certain: we were not, especially perhaps if we are members of the Outdoor Writers' Guild, designed to sit in front of a flickering screen tapping at a keyboard for hour after hour; or to sit in a metal box and propel ourselves, lemming-like, at 70 mph down a strip of concrete for mile after mile alongside thousands of others. Our bodies were designed to walk, run, climb and hunt for food out in the great outdoors; to sniff out and track an elusive prey or enemy, and to feel through our now underused senses imminent changes in the wind and the weather.

All these skills have been largely forgotten now, of course, and the only frisson of excitement or surge of adrenalin most of us gets is when we have a near miss on the motorway, or when we are watching an exciting game of football on television.

That is why I, and all the other contributors to this book, feel it is vitally important to re-establish that communion with nature, to pull on the boots and get out there to experience our wild country and all the vagaries of its weather. And if that means occasionally you feel an icy shiver of apprehension or uncertainty shooting up your spine as you push yourself that little bit harder on a severe climb, or realise that you may be lost in the encircling mists of a Pennine moor, that's exactly the point when you start actually to use the senses with which we were originally provided. With sudden realisation, you feel you are starting to live again, as you experience the true sense of re-creation.

marsh, Silverdale

This collection of 25 essays written and illustrated exclusively by members of the OWG, shows what an amazing variety of wild landscapes we are blessed with in the British Isles. From the storm-battered seastacks of St Kilda way out in the wild Atlantic, to the haunted creeks and misty marshes of the Norfolk Broads, and from the barren mountain heights of Snowdonia to the secret, sylvan forests of the High Weald, you can still experience and enjoy that well-worn and overused newspaper cliché – a walk on the wild side.

All OWG members were asked to suggest a place (a hill, island, dale or region) or a walk, climb, ride or paddle in a wild part of the British Isles which they would like to see in the book, either described or illustrated by themselves or someone else. Then 25 were selected for inclusion – one for each year of the OWG's life and to give a reasonable geographical spread – and the book is published by Rucksack Readers, which is run by yet another Guild member.

There were some surprises. For example, I hadn't realised how important islands – those enigmatic 'pieces of land' – were to so many people. We are an island race after all, and many members seem to feel the islands scattered around our coastline are the places where they most feel 'the call of the wild' today.

And there were one or two uncanny parallels, such as the enforced evacuations of the populations of St Kilda, Great Blasket, Achill Island and Connemara in the west of Ireland, at Diubaig on Skye and in the Upper Rheidol valley in mid-Wales. It's strange how places which were once inhabited but are now deserted somehow often feel lonelier than proper wildernesses. Something seems to linger in the air.

Walkers on the sands, Morecambe Bay

Dead tree, Ashdown Forest

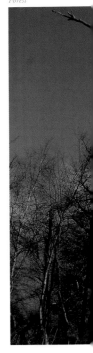

Encounters with wildlife are also obviously an important ingredient in the wilderness experience, whether it is being dive-bombed by great skuas on St Kilda or by Arctic terns on the Point of Ayr on the Isle of Man; a glimpse of a golden eagle in the Cairngorms, or hearing the weird 'whumph' of the secretive bittern, which echoes across the country from the Norfolk Broads to the marshes bordering Morecambe Bay.

There were surprises too, such as when internationally-renowned mountain photographer John Cleare plumped for the modest yet shapely Iron Age hill forts of Hambledon and Hod Hills, near his home in Wiltshire; and Alpine and Himalayan specialist Kev Reynolds chose the ancient forest of Ashdown, near his home in the Kentish Weald.

The Outdoor Writers' Guild – now usually abbreviated to OWG – was founded by a handful of outdoor gear writers who had congregated, as was their wont, around a hotel bar in Harrogate as they attended the annual trade show. Someone suggested that an association of writers who specialised in the outdoors would be a good idea, and the idea stuck.

Ice, Nant-y-llyn

In the early years, the membership of the Guild reflected the circumstances of its birth and consisted almost exclusively of gear writers and reviewers. But gradually, as walking and climbing literature expanded with new magazines and ever more publications, the emphasis switched to the wider constituency of magazine and guidebook authors and landscape photographers. Today, there are only a handful of gear specialists in the Guild – and as many professional photographers as there are writers.

The OWG has developed over the years into a well respected, responsible and professional organisation whose members range from landscape painters to wildlife experts. It produced a well-received and widely-distributed set of guidelines for the writers of footpath guides, which was included in our submission to the Government's Committee on the Environmental Impact of Leisure Activities in 1995. The then Countryside Commission was asked by Government to look into the feasibility of developing a scheme with the OWG to encourage 'greener' guidebooks which might, for example, deliberately exclude over-popular and therefore severely-eroded routes.

Stanage Edge

In 1990, as the newly-elected Chairman of the Guild, I introduced an annual system of awards for excellence in an attempt to encourage the highest standards and rewarding the best. Another award – originally known as the Golden Boot and now the OWG Crystal – still gives a nod to the Guild's genesis by recognising the most innovative new product or company in the outdoor trade.

But the most prized and prestigious annual award which the Guild makes is the Golden Eagle, an original painting by contributor David Bellamy, which goes to someone who has made a significant and lasting contribution to the outdoor world in general. Recipients have included such luminaries as Sir David Attenborough, the late Chris Brasher, Ken Wilson, Tom Weir and Alan Blackshaw.

The highlight of the Guild year is the AGM and Annual Dinner, at which the awards are presented. This has been held all round the country, from Norfolk to Dumfries and from Glasgow to Hereford, enabling the maximum number of members to attend. A travelling photographic exhibition of members' work has also toured the country to great critical acclaim.

As it enters its second quarter century, the OWG faces the future with confidence, secure in the knowledge that through its members' words and pictures, it is increasingly also becoming the medium through which many come vicariously to appreciate and enjoy the wonders of our precious wild country, and perhaps hear a whisper of Jack London's original 'call of the wild'.

Dunmore Head with distant Great Blasket, south-west Ireland

Finally I return, as I so often do, to John Muir. As I write this, there is a photograph of 'John of the Mountains' on my office wall. It acts a constant reminder that, to quote from *Our National Parks* again: 'To the sane and free it will hardly seem necessary to cross the continent in search of wild beauty, however easy the way, for they find it in abundance wherever they chance to be.'

Citing Thoreau with his 'little oases of wildness in the desert of our civilisation', and echoing William Blake's famous couplet:
To see a World in a Grain of Sand,
And a Heaven in a Wild Flower

Muir added: 'Like Thoreau, they see forests in orchards and patches of huckleberry bush, and oceans in ponds and drops of dew. Few in these hot, dim, strenuous times are quite sane or free; choked with care like clocks full of dust, laboriously doing so much good and making so much money – or so little – they are no longer good for themselves.'

Cashtal yn Ard Stones,
Isle of Man

Launching from Bhat
blink of houses west of Cal.

Scotland

Hamish Brown
1 The last wild place: St Kilda

Long before Napes Needle was climbed and rock climbing became a pastime, young men were already active. In the 19th century, a party of men from Ness (Lewis) crossed the Minch to make the first ascent of the Great Stack of Handa, in Sutherland, a 'raid' with exactly the same one-upmanship behind it as was climbing 'Sassenach' on the Ben over a century later. And the feat has only been repeated once, by Tom Patey, in 1967. But it is of remoter, wilder stacks I want to write.

The men of St Kilda climbed not only of necessity but for the same display of macho virility that the species has always portrayed. So long had they been doing so that St Kildans developed larger, more able feet (perhaps a *Homo sapiens pediatum* alongside the island's own variant mouse and wren?). This of course was long before modern climbing equipment, such as PAs, rockboots or even tricouni nails, were invented.

Ropes were used, hefty horsehair ropes, and if safety aids were conspicuously absent, their daring was the more remarkable for that. You don't take more than one unprotected fall on the cliffs and stacks of St Kilda. Stac Biorach stands as a sheer pillar in the sea between Hirta and Soay and was climbed by a lad to win a wager (a pouch of tobacco) off a visitor. What could sound more contemporary?

ouses and cleits, Kilda

eits, Mullach More king to Village Bay, Kilda

Soay from Am Cambir

Young men wanting a wife displayed their prowess by perching on the Lover's Stone, a cannon of rock jutting over space. He took position at the end of the stone with just a heel on the rock, placing his other foot on the first and his fists on that, an awkward crouch which you might like to try on the bottom step of a stair. Holding the position for a minute was the requisite.

The ascents of Stac Lee in modern times could be counted on the fingers of one hand, yet it was climbed annually for culling gugas – young gannets – a vital winter food which was stored in the drystane cleits – beehive-shaped stone-built storehouses. Stac Boreray is larger and even had some of these airy shelters on it, which was just as well. A dog was left behind one year and survived to greet the guga collectors the following season.

In 1759 the boat which was returning with the culled birds was smashed on the rocks in Village Bay and the crew drowned. There was no other boat on Hirta (where the village lay) so nothing was done till the following June when the factor made his annual visit. The marooned men were then rescued, having survived a winter on that most wild and inhospitable rock – an amazing story of survival.

The first tourist vessel to visit the islands was in 1838 and an endless succession followed, for the island attracted geologists and botanists as well as those coming to gawk. It reminds me of an old Skye man who said 'We only have two industries in Skye; the sheep and the tourists. And we fleece the both of them'.

Seton Gordon visited in 1927 and while preparing the anthology, *Seton Gordon's Scotland* (Whittles, July 2005), I was able to see his archive pictures of his stay and of a scary visit to Soay. The first tourist ascent of Boreray was in 1902.

Soay sh

Over the years there were many tragedies at sea. In 1863, eight people lost their lives en route to Harris. Periodic shipwrecks on St Kilda or Rockall saw survivors succoured by the generosity of the islanders to the extent that they themsleves were left starving. On one such occasion when relief arrived on the Saturday, unloading had to wait till Monday in order not to break the strict Sabbath observance.

Sometimes visitors brought fatal infectious diseases. Smallpox in 1727-28 caused 94 deaths leaving just four adults and 26 youngsters. Three men and eight boys were marooned on Stac an Armin, and so kept free of infection.

Many visitors wrote books following their voyages. Having been owned since 1956 by the National Trust for Scotland, the village has been partially restored and much surveyed. I once had the happy remit to take a cleit to bits and rebuild it to study just how the St Kildans had done so.

St Kilda lies forty miles out in the Atlantic beyond the Hebrides, yet it has some of the oldest houses to be discovered by archaeologists in Scotland. For thousands of years the sea was the country's great 'highway' while the land was rock, forest and bog. To live on the edge of the world, however, still required a special sort of people and it is not surprising that climbing cliffs became part of their lives – some of it done for fun. This tradition deserves better recognition.

The highest summit on Hirta is Conachair, 430 m (1410 ft) and from it the highest cliff in the country plunges to the sea. The bald dome is frequently scoured by gales yet I have bivvied by the cairn in a balmy calm to observe night-flying petrels and watch a 'rosy fingered dawn'. This is one of those special places that lure the adventurous back, and I have been lucky to make several visits. The inevitable seasickness is a modest price to pay.

The shrewish Lady Grange who threatened to inform on her Jacobite husband was kidnapped and spent between 1734 and 1742 a prisoner on St Kilda. She tried to smuggle out letters in rolls of tweed or float off a 'mailboat' message. In 1746, soldiers combed the island for the fugitive Prince Charlie.

The 'mailboat' was simply a message sent by sea to wherever it might land, usually secreted in some waterproof container and attached to a bladder. On at least one occasion it effectively brought relief during a famine following a harvest failure. NTS workparties re-enact this ploy and 'mailboats' have come ashore all round the Scottish coast and even in Norway. One of mine landed in Harris, four days after launching.

I once took an American party onto Dun, the island which lies like a panhandle to Village Bay. Being sentimental naturalists, they watched in horror as 'bonxies' (great skuas) grabbed puffins and kept shoving their heads under water till they drowned. St Kilda is not a tame world.

Sadly, life became intolerable in more modem times and the population was evacuated in 1930. It was only a few years ago that the last of the evacuees died in Morven, where the people from barren, treeless Hirta were settled by the government – to work for the Forestry Commission.

Sunrise over the stacks of St Kilda

Judy Armstrong

2 *Another day in paradise: Outer Hebrides*

Silence.

A niggle of wind. A wand of grass taps my tent and a wave sips the shore. A fine, white shimmy of powdered shells creaks as I stand to stare across the bay. I sigh, fat with happiness, on my Hebridean island.

My beach is on Little Berneray, an island off the northern tip of Great Berneray, itself an island off the western coast of Lewis. This is a land of fantasy beaches, black-rock mountains and complex coastlines battered by Atlantic winds.

Once a remote toehold for Picts and Norsemen, these Outer Hebridean islands were later cleared of humans to make way for sheep. Now they are home to tenacious communities whose way of life has won out over hardship and isolation.

It is a wild place. Hen harriers swoop low, road signs warn 'Caution! Otters Crossing', restored blackhouses sprout thatched roofs, flowers sway over dunes and beaches. And always there is the sea: cobalt blue, clear as ice.

channel near Bostadh, between Great and Little Berneray

Ah, the sea. It jiggles in a crazy dance around this strip of land, and some stretches are safer than others, especially in a slender kayak. Some paddlers seek out surf, but I like my kayaking calm. I hunted around, and found that the sheltered bays of Lewis and Harris would be my passport to Hebridean adventure.

We became a team of three: Duncan, my paddling partner, and I were joined by Tim, a Londoner transplanted to Stornoway. We met near the Callanish Stones, the Hebrides' answer to Stonehenge. Tall stone slabs, textured by centuries, make up a ring, a line, a cross, or a muddle, depending on where you stand. We wandered among them, watching the shadows.

Our launch site was Bhaltos, a blink of houses to the west of Callanish. With kayaks loaded, sleek and heavy, we eased onto a calm sea. Caves boomed with the tide, gannets power-dived for fish and chocolate razorbills bobbed on a slinky swell. The compass was set for Great Pabay, an island of sand and rock, an immense natural arch and a secret lagoon.

We landed on a silver beach and pitched our tents below the ruins of a chapel. From the highest point of the island we won views of mainland Lewis, then walked over the arch to watch the sea boiling below. The summer sun never really set that night, just dipped vaguely toward the horizon before beginning its upward curve. Welcome to a new day, it said, another day in paradise.

Tackling waves on the coast of Berneray

Callanish St[...] the Hebrides' ans[...] to Stoneh[...]

We crossed to Berneray and the days floated by. Coasting out of a small lagoon, Tim spotted a head in the sea. Otter? Maybe. Mink, maybe. Fat seals flopped on rocks and skuas swooped. The sheltered bay of Tobson lured us in for lunch, the turquoise sea flickering with light, the beach a pearly white. We scrambled over the headland to view the way forward; Tim and Duncan dropped to their bellies on a cliff-top and looked into the eyes of a nesting fulmar. Perched on the black wall of a coastal cleft, she was surrounded by pink flowers and yellow lichen, in an idyllic maritime nursery.

At the top of the island we found Bostadh, the Iron Age settlement buried under sand and discovered in 1992, when a storm blew the beach clean. In the valley at the beach's edge was a low building with a thatched roof, a replica of an Iron Age house, faithfully reproduced. Inside, down steep stone steps, we met Elizabeth Macleod, the guide here since the house opened in 1999.

The house was divided into two, in a wonky figure of eight; it had a dirt floor, holes for smoke to escape and a rickety ladder leading into a roof space. A fire glowed in the centre of the room. 'Usually I do some baking here – oatcakes or a little broth – just to give the atmosphere,' Elizabeth told us.

A blue smoke haze drifted around the beams and a shaft of light burned a hole on the stone wall. It moved with the smoke, like a laser beam, in a surreal mix of past and future. From Bostadh, the sea pulled us past salmon farms to the uninhabited island of Little Berneray. Once enough people lived here for a school to flourish, but now only kayakers and a herd of Highland cattle, take advantage of the solitude.

We camped above a white beach, below a chapel and burial ground. As the sun sank low I climbed the hill to investigate. The names Macleod, MacDonald and Maclennan covered stone triangles, a lopsided cross and weather-beaten slabs. I leaned against the chapel wall. The water shimmered and the silence sang in my head. I closed my eyes, draw a deep breath, and absorbed the Hebridean night.

We spent a week in the bays around Berneray before skipping across to Harris and the crystal waters of Loch Resort. It's a wild, wild place, home to sea eagles and huge swells riding in from the Atlantic. We kept it tight, sliding in from the Hushinish jetty, a concrete tongue prodding tentatively at the sea. It was a short glide to Scarp, a rugged island freckled with ruined blackhouses. Climbing the highest hill, we saw clear to St Kilda, its islands like the spine of a pale blue dinosaur.

From here we could see our next campsite, a wedge of gold sand between turquoise sea and green-grey hills. To reach it, we caught a current which swept us past Scarp and around a headland into Loch Cravadale. A guillemot, heavy with sand eels, bobbed before our boats. A tern dived and a raft of jellyfish squelched under my bow, translucent and slow.

The beach, when we landed, was flush with wild flowers. We stripped the kayaks of their cargo: fresh, fleshy scallops and sea-cooled white wine. As the sun dipped we ate and drank, watched the mountains change colour, and listened to the evening. Small waves sighed on the beach… rolled in, rolled out, rolled in… oyster catchers strutted and tutted, as the surf beat a rhythm on the sand.

And later, silence. I sighed, fat with happiness, on my Hebridean island.

On Harris, looking down to Loch Crabhadail

Chris Mitchell

3 *Alone with nature: Loch Diubaig, Skye*

'Look, I'm in a hurry. I have a Munro to climb… What did you want to
show me?… Just a short walk? Twenty minutes to the coast and back?…
A sea loch, sorry? – I didn't quite catch the name… And why are we
whispering?'

The place is Loch Diubaig on the Isle of Skye. Take the side road to
Greshornish House Hotel, off the main Portree to Dunvegan road. A farm
track leads to a rough path which takes you around the edge of wet moorland
along low coastal cliffs to the head of the loch. You won't have been here
before. It's nowhere near the Cuillin – miles away from a Munro… and we
are whispering because otters live here.

Wave surge on Loch Diubaig

Wear something quiet if you can – waterproofs that don't rustle, preferably with drab colours. Wash off any aftershave or scent. Pack an extra fleece and take a hat, scarf and gloves. Forget all the usual walk descriptions of familiar places. This is not about reaching a summit to admire the view, or striding out to cover great distances. This is about being alone with nature.

Stand here on the edge of this beach in January on a stormy day with a Force 9 blowing straight out of the north. Look at the map. Loch Diubaig on the north coast of Skye is the focal point of a giant rock funnel. A north wind produces a wave-surge that begins far out in The Minch, and like the River Severn with its famous bore, causes an increase in wave height, only this wave-surge keeps coming as each giant roller crashes in between narrowing side walls. It feels dangerous, even on land.

But today, all is quiet and you can understand why people once settled here. That was a time when a sense of place was more important than a mobile phone signal. Diubaig's deserted village is just to your left. There are still no roads to penetrate this hidden sanctuary. A special place – and a sad place, for here are the graves of a local family who chose a raised area at the head of the loch for their final resting-place. The middle of three stone memorials marks the grave of a child who died when only one year old. The parents are buried on either side.

Evening solitude, Loch Diubaig

Graves on the loch shore

Otter swimming in late evening light

Walk down the coast and stand on the edge of the now-calm sea. Focus your eyes north to the Outer Isles. It is early spring and it is dusk. The physicist notes a temperature drop of five degrees and the air is so still that an inversion has developed in Loch Snizort. A layer of warm air has been trapped on the sea surface forming a shimmering band of haze. The edges of the islands curve back underneath themselves. The low parts disappear. A fishing boat is cut in half and its mast and top-lights appear upside down in the haze. The physicist mumbles something about an 'inferior mirage'. These things are rare and not easily forgotten.

And then it is June. Clear as a bell. Now focus your eyes straight down the loch to Uig. You can see the houses arranged above the harbour; see the gleaming white Cal-Mac ferry returning from Tarbert on Harris. But this is Loch Diubaig, cut off from Loch Greshornish, in the inner reach of Loch Snizort – far away from the busy tourist routes. On this cool summer day, the air is so still the poet can hear the barnacles breathing. The biologist hears only crustaceans clamping shut in response to his moving shadow.

The tide is out, leaving a tangled field of kelp studded with blue-rayed limpets – an impossible blue, as if someone has drawn lines on the shells with a fluorescent pen. On the faint breeze you can smell the ozone. The air is so fresh – the modern nose is assaulted by the freshness of it all. Where is this place? What is this? Colours that can't exist, a scent never experienced before. There are no reference points inside the modern brain to make sense of this primeval landscape.

High on the shore, the geologist sees a 25-foot raised beach. The botanist finds lilac flowers of thrift and sea milkwort. On the basalt rock along the high water line there is a startling band of black lichen that changes to gold and then grey as you walk away from the sea. This is the route the otters take.

As you cross the shore, you reach a raised platform of sea-washed turf. Here, a freshwater pool is fed by a maze of narrow streams. Look closely at the mound by the side of the pool, the one that looks like a large green thimble. See the fragments of crab claws, now weathered pink; the bits of backbone from pollock and mackerel, each vertebra shaped like a miniature diablo. There are streaks of black slime with a scent strong enough to keep rival males away. A faint line of flattened grass can be seen leading into the pool, before emerging on the other side. It leads to another mound with yet more fish bones.

These mounds have been formed by generations of otters. Their 'spraints' (droppings) have built up over time leaving a territorial network of dark green patches. Twenty minutes spent here and you feel the human senses are being re-tuned to this ancient world. You begin to read the signs. Twenty minutes so easily becomes half a day.

That's Loch Diubaig: a link with the past; a place to slow down and forget the clock; to recharge the batteries and heighten the senses; room enough for the scientist and the poet to experience total solitude as well as the elemental forces of nature.

Freshwater outflow with sprainting mound at centre

Chris Townsend

4 Symbols of the wild: Northern Cairgorms

Swirling snow fills the sky, washing in great waves across the mountain. There is no horizon; no up, no down. Land and sky merge into nothingness. Only the crunch of boots into snow, the solidity of the packed whiteness underfoot, feels real.

Turning, I look back to see my companion, startling bright in his red and blue clothing, all other colour bleached from the world. Head down, hood up, snow goggles covering his eyes, he climbs steadily in my boot prints, thrusting ski poles into the snow for support at every stride. Glancing at the compass grasped clumsily in my gloved hand, I continue on up this invisible mountain.

Loch Morlich in a storm

Coire an t-Sneachda
in winter

Righ
Loch Mallachie
Abernethy Forest, at dus

Suddenly there is definition in the storm, an ice-encrusted edifice rises above us, seemingly towering into the sky. 'We're there,' I call back. My companion is unconvinced. Fooled by the lack of scale, he thinks we are facing a much steeper slope. We're not.

The edifice is the ice-encrusted weather station on the summit of Cairn Gorm, recording some of the wildest weather in Britain. A quick snack and a gulp of hot liquid from our flasks and we are on our way again, half-walking, half-sliding down the mountain, sinking into thigh-deep drifts then skidding on patches of rippled ice.

Slowly the falling snow eases and the mist begins to dissolve, giving hints of a world beyond the bubble of hazy white that encloses us, the edges of which are always twenty feet away and which we never reach. As the bubble softens and dissipates a dizzying sense of space comes and goes.

Far below a loch shines briefly then the mist closes in again and it's gone. Another break in the barrier and there's a dark forest filling the hole. Then suddenly a rush of cold wind rips the remaining clouds to tatters, sending them spinning away to melt in the air. Horizons race into the distance as space expands dramatically.

This new world is vast and startling. Steep snow-streaked cliffs drop into a deep armchair-shaped hollow, its arms, long rocky ridges. This is Coire an t-Sneachda, the Corrie of the Snows. The white snowy world turns dark beyond the corrie, dark with the Scots pines of Glenmore and Rothiemurchus forests, the largest remaining remnants of the ancient Wood of Caledon, spreading along the feet of the high mountains, creeping up the lower hillsides and encircling the icy waters of Loch Morlich.

*   *   *

It is another day. We are in the forest. It is spring not winter, and the snows are gone from the woodland floor. Great Caledonian pines rise from bosses of spreading roots, looking like the gnarled digits of ancient hands. The curving, twisted branches shade the ground. The bark of these old trees is grey and deeply grooved, their trunks crooked, knobbly and twisted. Around them younger, much younger pines, rise straight and tall, their trunks and branches glowing red in the bright sunlight. These are the future, the regenerating forest reclaiming its land.

Part of the redness moves, skips suddenly from one tree to the next. It's a red squirrel, a common but always delightful sight in these woods. We watch as it pauses on a branch to glance warily towards us, its bushy tail curled over its back, then it's gone in a quick, spiralling scamper up the tree trunk.

Moving on we stride through clumps of blaeberry and cowberry with shining bright green leaves. Later in the summer the former will provide delicious bitter-sweet purple berries which stain the hands and lips.

In clearings, heather grows along with dark green straggling juniper bushes. Stands of delicate-seeming birch trees with fresh green leaves and rippling silver bark break up the solid green of the pine forest. Every so often mounds of pine needles are heaped up in an orderly fashion. Peer closely at these: the surface is alive and moving with wood ants, who live here.

A stream rushes through the forest, sparkling over stones and deepening into dark pools. The water leads to Loch an Eilein, a wide sweep of silver water stretching out to more trees and then the brown, snow-streaked hills. Heading upwards we plunge through soft mounds of vegetation, meandering carefully around fallen trees and mossy boulders.

As we climb the rocky slopes the trees thin and dwindle, until the last few matted, contorted clumps lie close to the ground to avoid the biting wind. This is the natural tree line, now sadly rare in Britain. Free of the forest, we walk more easily up grey-brown, stony slopes to a broad ridge.

A small cairn marks the highest summit, Sgor Gaoith, the Peak of the Winds. Reaching it is startling, disorientating, inspiring and exhilarating, for it is perched right on the brink of a precipitous drop, shattered rock ridges and broken cliffs leading down, down to the distant dark waters of Loch Einich, almost two thousand feet below. The loch fills a narrow valley head, its sides a tangled mass of crags, gullies and scree slopes split by the silver threads of streams.

Across from Sgor Gaoith the stony slopes rise steadily to the bulky summit of mighty Braeriach, one of the great hills of the Cairngorms. As we stare at the mountains a speck in the sky grows and soars, sweeping over the slopes: a golden eagle, the symbol of the wild.

*   *   *

Later that spring I am back in the forest again, walking beside another loch, this one with a name also redolent of wildness. This is Loch Garten, and it was in the forest here that in 1954 ospreys returned to nest in Britain for the first time in almost forty years. Every year ospreys come back to nest at Loch Garten. Every year I go back too, to see the ospreys, to feel their presence and to renew the sense that this is a wild place, a special place, a place to care for and care about, a place that restores the soul.

This is the Cairngorms. This is the wild.

The ruined castle, Loch an Eilein

Roly Smith

5 *Columba's tears: Port na Curaich, Iona*

Silhouetted against the sunset from the summit of Ben More on Mull, Iona seems to float like a vision set in a wave-beaten sea of shimmering gold. It recalls the Hebridean legend of Tir nan Og – the land of the ever-young – which always lies, temptingly unattainable, over the western horizon.

This tiny island – it measures only three miles by one – is still regarded by many as the jewel of the Inner Hebrides. As the greatest connoisseur of the Scottish mountain scene, the late W H Murray pointed out, Iona seems to have a purity of light and colour which exceeds all the others. 'Tiree has equal clarity of air but not of colour, which in Iona invades even her seas' he wrote in The Hebrides. 'One's first and abiding impression is of greenness and fairness, and of a grace peculiar to the union in one small island of a multiplicity of minor excellences.'

Most of Iona is made up of banded Lewisian gneiss which, at around 2,800 million years old, is among the oldest rock anywhere on Earth. At places like Columba's Bay on the south-eastern tip of the island, the kaleidoscope of colours – from deep reds to purples, greens and blacks – of the wave-washed stones is simply breathtaking. But the most prized pebbles of all are those of the white, lime-green serpentine-flecked Ionan marble, known locally as 'St Columba's Tears'.

*t na Curaich –
'port of the coracle'*

*Port na Curaich and
St Columba's Bay,
towards Colonsay*

*St Ronan's
and the vill*

Three centuries ago, Martin Martin had observed in his *Description of the Western Isles of Scotland* (1695): 'These pretty variegated stones in the shoar…ripen to a green colour, and are then proper for Carving. The Natives say these stones are Fortunate, but only for some particular thing, which the Person thinks fit to name, in exclusion of everything else.'

*   *   *

The best way to appreciate the varied colours and the true wildness of Iona is to take the boggy paths across the Sliabh Siar, the rocky spine of Lewisian gneiss which makes up the backbone of the island, to reach the stony beach known as Port na Curaich, the 'port of the coracle'. This is the legendary spot where St Columba, or Colum Cille – poet, prophet and sage – landed with 12 followers in his skin-covered boat in disgrace and exile from his native Ireland in AD 563. He had sailed towards the then heathen Hebrides to light the lamp of that special brand of iconoclastic Celtic Christianity which was soon to illuminate the whole of pagan Europe.

The easiest route to the twin pebble beaches of Port na Curaich and Port an Fhir-Bhreige ('the port of the false man') is by way of the east-west road which rises over the fertile central plain of the island from the sheltered, sandy bays of the east coast.

Passing the rough hay meadow of Lagnagiogan ('the hollow of the thistles') on a still summer evening, you may hear, as I have, the unmistakeable grating call of the elusive corncrake; a sound exactly like passing your fingernail over the teeth of a comb. Even on these specially-managed meadows, you are much more likely to hear the corncrake than ever to see this skulking master of camouflage.

You drop down to the dazzling, snow-white sands of Camus Cul an t-Saimh – 'the bay at the back of the ocean' – across the broad grassy sward of the machair (now the links of the Iona Golf Club) and then turn south up a rough track, passing the island's only remaining natural loch – Loch Staonaig.

Thread your way through the rocky, heather-covered outcrops of venerable grey gneiss down into verdant greensward of Lag Odhar – the brown hollow – which is often occupied by a contented herd of cattle. Here and there in the damper spots, patches of the golden, heraldic fleur-de-lis flags of iris – another Ionan speciality – enliven the pastoral scene as you descend to the beach where Columba landed 1400 years ago.

Once ashore, he climbed to the nearest high point above the beach, the heather-covered hill known as Carn Cul ri Eirinn – the cairn of the back to Ireland – and cast his eyes south and west to check if he could still see his beloved homeland. He could not, but it must have been a typically misty day. The hills of Ireland are in fact just visible in exceptionally good conditions from the summit cairn, 80 miles away to the south-west beyond Colonsay and Islay. Carn Cul ri Eirinn is still one of the finest and wildest viewpoints on Iona.

I was last there on a hazy late summer's day, when Ireland was well beyond even the most optimistic of gazes. Beyond the pristine white strand of Camus Cul an t-Saimh, the view extended north over the floating sombrero of the Dutchman's Cap, Lunga and the columnar cliffs of Staffa to the low hills of Tiree and Coll, floating like a mirage above the millpond Atlantic. I found a smooth, wave-rounded pebble of Ionan marble near the summit cairn, and it now occupies pride of place on my bookshelves. I also always carry a small polished piece of Iona marble with me in Martin's particularly held local belief that anyone who does so will never be involved in a shipwreck nor drown. So far, it seems to have worked.

Nearby but notoriously difficult to find is the green strath of Liana an Tairbh, which leads off to the east of Lag Odhar and down past the elder-haunted ruins of Tobhta nan Sassunaich – 'the house of the lowlanders (or Englishmen)'. From here you pass more ruins of Tigh nan Gall ('house of the strangers') where at times the drone of the pipes can still sometimes be heard on the sighing wind, and then steeply down a narrow defile into the secret, lost world of the Iona Marble Quarry.

This is another of Iona's surprises, for here, tucked away in one of the wildest and most remote spots on the island, are the creaking, rusting remains of industry. The Duke of Argyll oversaw the quarrying and transporting out by sea of the prized green-veined marble from the late 18th century until the early 20th century. You can still see evidence of the last unsuccessful attempts in the abandoned remains of the black-painted Gloucester-made gas engine installed in 1911, which powered the machinery of the Sassenachs. Alongside the engine, water tanks and cutting frame, cut blocks of the gleaming stone tumble in great heaps below the glistening quarry face and out into the translucent, restless sea.

Columba was well known for his piety and love of the simple life, and I wonder whether his marbled tears might have flowed at this industrialisation of his holy island. You can never quite escape the spirit of Columba on Iona, and he is attributed with this much-quoted poem, in which he could well have been referring to Port na Curaich:

In Iona of my heart, Iona of my love,
Instead of monks' voices shall be the lowing of cattle;
But ere the world come to an end,
Iona shall be as it was.

Evening light on
Port Fhir-Bhreige

Rennie McOwan

6 Hill of ghosts: Dumyat, Ochils

Legend has it that when that old grey wanderer of the hills wraps his cloak of mist around the summits of the mountains, then people of the past can seem to re-appear.

In the case of my favourite childhood hill, that would mean a rich galaxy of spectral beings; the spear-carrying Picts who build a fort on a lower shoulder; the probing Roman patrols who erected a marching camp not far away; writers like Sir Walter Scott, who brought the hill into one of his epic poems, and the youthful Robert Louis Stevenson, who spent holidays nearby and whose ascent of this special peak influenced his descriptions of topography in one of his most famous books, *Treasure Island*.

Shadowy men and women accused of being warlocks and witches lived nearby, and the early tweed-clad mountaineers, including the pioneering Harold Raeburn, came to explore the big rock faces and found, alas, friable cliffs for the most part unsuitable for climbing.

This much-loved hill is called Dumyat (pronounced 'Dum-eye-at'), a name which is generally taken to mean the dun (or fort) of the Myaetae, a prominent Pictish tribe.

myat from Craigomas
oss Menstrie Glen

Dumyat is a frontier hill. It stands at the west end of the Ochils (pronounced 'Oh-chil,' with the 'ch' as in loch), a long, mainly grassy range which takes its name from the Celtic uchel, the high ground. The Ochils lie just north of the meandering River Forth in central Scotland. At 1376 feet (418 m) Dumyat is not particularly high, but to us wandering children, it was most certainly wild.

The steep southern escarpment of the Ochils is known to geologists as the Ochils Fault. The sea once lapped against forest-clad slopes here and the remains of whales and oyster beds have been found.

This mountain wall is the true boundary between Highlands and Lowlands and the hill names of Dumyat and the Ochils tell of a meeting place of different cultures. They derive from five languages, old and 'modern' Gaelic, Scots, Brittonic and English, and sometimes they are a mixture of several and therefore difficult to unravel.

I was brought up in a now rapidly-growing little village called Menstrie and from my bedroom window I could see a little, grassy hill called Craigomas and just behind it the jutting cliffs of Dumyat. It was our playground and once we had done our 'messages' (errands), we headed for nearby Menstrie Wood, the curving Menstrie Glen and its chuckling burns and the slopes of Dumyat.

My youthful memories were of the clean scent of water soaked moss, lichen and stones, of the heady smells of summer, of the burgeoning heather and of birch, willow and hazel in spring. The sounds were the cackling jackdaws which nested in rabbit holes, the croak of the occasional carrion crow or raven and, on the higher ground, the burbling call of the curlew, the cackle of the grouse and the musical piping of the golden plover, known in Gaelic as feadan, the (bagpipes) chanter. I was accustomed to the crying of sheep and lambs, the barking of dogs, the swish of the wind in the long grass, and at night, the eerie, shrieking cry of the vixen fox.

From Dumyat summit towards the shoulder of the

Looking south from Dumyat, s

The names in the gorge sections of the glen told us of past human activity: the Washing Linn (a pool with flat rocks) and the Jeely Pot, a deep pool shaped like a jam jar. In the burn, we built turf and stone dams to deepen the small dark pools and could sometimes manage a few strokes in them and occasionally 'guddle' small trout by cornering them in the shallows. The pools are smaller now because the flow of the burn was reduced in recent years by the enlarging of a small reservoir further up the glen and known as the Loss Dam (from the Gaelic lios, a fertile place).

A ruined farmhouse called Jerah at the 'back' of Dumyat and Menstrie Glen possibly gets its name from the Gaelic dearg (pronounced 'jerrak') because of red scree nearby. There was a family in this house when I was a boy and further back, it was reputed to be the home of a warlock and the haunt of faeries.

The back of Dumyat rises in north-facing grass and heather slopes from Menstrie Glen burn and its small feeder burns. There was once human habitation here too, because when light snow covers the ground the faint outline of houses, pens and cultivation strips can be seen.

The steep burns of the Ochils were ideal for turning mill wheels and the hills became sheep country. Weaving communities sprang up along the southern base and at the western foot of Dumyat there stands a little conservation village called Blairlogie, which for a time became a kind of health spa to which people travelled to drink goats' milk.

The summit of Dumyat provides one of the most spectacular vistas in Scotland. Behind flat or rolling farm and moorland stand many of the main peaks of the Highland Line – Stuc a' Chroin, Ben Vorlich, Ben Each, Ben Ledi, Ben Venue, the Gargunnock and Touch (pronounced 'tooch') hills, the Campsies and the Fintry hills. Another turn gives wide views into the main green and tawny mass of the Ochils and along the fault escarpment.

Dumyat has been called the teacher's hill, because from its summit, the hill stravaiger (wanderer) can see many layers of history. Southward lies a broad, flat plain, dotted with farms, towns and villages and close by are strategic Stirling and its famous castle; the towering 19th century monument to the Braveheart patriot, William Wallace; the modern buildings of the 'new' University of Stirling, and the far-off outlines of the Cleish and Saline hills in Kinross, the fringes of the Fife Lomonds, the Pentlands near Edinburgh and the Moorfoots even further south. The lower ground around Stirling was once the cockpit of Scotland and the sites of seven battlefields can be seen.

Old, now abandoned, coal mines operated on the plain and prospectors for silver and copper left their mark on the hill. The summit is marked with an obsolete trig point, plus a brazier erected to celebrate a royal jubilee and a concrete replica of the cap badge of the Argyll and Sutherland Highlanders, the local regiment. Many lovers of Dumyat feel we could do without all three because they dilute the wilderness quality of the hill.

The Scottish writer, traveller and radical politician R B Cunninghame Graham, known as Don Roberto because of his travels in Latin America, was once on a hill in Paraguay when he met up with another horseman on the summit. He was a stranger to him, but he knew by the man's accent that he was Scottish and commended the view. The stranger replied: 'Aye, man, but it doesn't beat the view from Dumyat'.

Clutter on the summit of Dumyat

Nick Jenkins

7 *Oneness with the world: Isle of Man*

I suspect that many readers have heard of the Isle of Man, and may have even pledged to visit it one day, but have not yet made it across the sea. It is one of those places that people are aware of but, other than the world famous motor bike TT races, know very little about. This was certainly the case with me before I had an opportunity to visit the Island (or Mainland, as Manx folk call it) to explore it for myself.

Niarbyl Bay, Isle of Man

Lighthouse, Point of Ayre

I am primarily a landscape photographer and, on first arriving, I wasn't quite sure what sort of landscapes the island could offer. My concerns could not have been more misplaced – it was all there. Rugged coastlines, remote high heath and moorland, and above all, a real feeling of solitude and peace. True, the biking events attract thousands of spectators, but had I not read about them I would have had no reason to suppose that such events ever took place. It only took me a day or two to realise that this was indeed a very good place to be.

Waterfall, Glen M

The island is particularly special to me for one good reason; it manages to combine both spectacular and rugged coastlines with remote inland hills and moors. Either landscape can be explored at will, often without seeing another soul. And because at its extremities Man only measures 32 miles by 13, the distances between these two are within the walking capacity of most reasonably fit people, giving anyone the chance to truly 'escape'. And the only way to get under the skin of this wonderfully empty place is to put on your boots, shoulder your rucksack and walk.

For me, it is the coastline of the Isle which really appeals. There is an excellent footpath, the Raad ny Foillan, or Way of the Gull, which works its way right around the coastline, passing through some breathtaking coastal scenery. The nature and geology of the coast is extremely varied, ranging from high gorse and heather-clad hills falling steep to the rocks and the Irish Sea below, to long, wide and totally deserted sandy beaches. Add to this the wild and remote northerly tip of Point of Ayre (Ayre is Manx Gaelic for a gravel beach), with its vast limestone shingle banks and colony of terns.

Perhaps one of the most spiritual places is the headland of Niarbyl. Not difficult to access either by lane or footpath, it is nonetheless entirely remote with a wonderful sense of intimacy. Niarbyl was used as a key location for gentle cult comedy film *Waking Ned*, on the basis that the wild coastline hereabouts closely resembles that of the west coast of Ireland, fitting the storyline of the film.

I sat on the rocks one glorious afternoon, just taking it all in. The low sun picked up the crashing waves beautifully, adding a sparkle which resembled a scattering of diamonds across a rough, heaving sea. Gulls wheeled overhead and in the distance, a remote cottage lay sheltered under the hill rising high behind it. The rocky cliffs receded in front of me, becoming more blue and hazy as the distance increased. I had sought out the headland to photograph it but, at this precise moment, I was perfectly content to sit and simply absorb the beauty.

There was no desire to rush to get the camera mounted onto the tripod that afternoon. It would almost have felt disrespectful: to photograph this place would be to try to rationalise, sanitise or tame it. Eventually, of course, I relented and took photographs from as many angles as possible. And I left Niarbyl with a real sense of hiraeth – the Welsh word which roughly means 'longing'. I will be back.

The following day saw me exploring the vast shingle bank of Point of Ayre on the northernmost tip of Man. Never could two sections of coastline offer such a marked contrast. Here was wide open space, a huge pebble beach sloping right down to the sea, and backed by flat grassy heathland. Here there was no protection from the wind, and more terns than I could readily contemplate.

I was accompanied to Point of Ayre by Tony, an OWG writer colleague who, in his own way, was equally absorbed by this wide open place. Simply to sit on the pebbles, to listen to the crashing of the distant waves and to be constantly deafened by the wild cries of the Arctic terns was special. Again, before rushing to try and capture the scene on film I slowed right down, trying to imagine that I was becoming a part of this wild and truly remote spot and seeking out the spirit of the place.

Meanwhile, back to harsh reality, my colleague wandered onto the beach to explore while I just sat, watching, observing. My reverie was rudely interrupted, however, as he had blundered into the birds' home territory and they were exacting their revenge in no uncertain fashion. I never really knew whether Tony was waving his white handkerchief to indicate surrender or to attempt to mop the blood from his pecked head. You don't mess with Arctic terns.

It is all too easy to think of the Isle of Man as being a pocket version of mainland UK, but to do so would be doing the island a grave injustice. Remote and wild places always help to engender a feeling of oneness with our environment but, on Man, this goes one stage further. Not only does the island impart that wonderful feeling of being away from it all, which we so often need to re-charge our batteries in this increasingly frantic society, but the very fact that Man is an island just adds, for me, that very special ingredient of solitude.

Cliffs at Silverda

*Cashtal yn Ard
Chambered Tomb*

England

Anthony Toole

8 A reluctant wilderness: Whitfield Moor, Northumbria

The South Tyne valley does not advertise itself, and even can appear reluctant to receive visitors. Yet it gets its share of walkers, for the Pennine Way follows most of its course. Nevertheless, it is pushed into the south-west corner of Northumberland, squeezed between high moorlands and seems less accessible than the rest of the county.

Sphagnum pool, Whitfield Moor summit in background

e Beck below Black, Cross Fell

Whitfield Lough from summit cairn

It was nearly midday when I left Slaggyford, taking the Barhaugh road for a short distance, then turning through the farmyard at Williamston and up the public bridleway toward Parson Shields. Where the track forked, I followed the higher path, past hawthorns and rowans in full berry.

A ruined building marked the corner of a field above the first rise. A pair of buzzards circled overhead. At the far side of the field, a farmworker was mending a gap in the drystone wall. He was not hopeful of his work surviving, as the previous foundations had been washed away by a spring which still bubbled out of the hillside just above the wall. He had built a small conduit through the base, which he hoped might prolong the life of his repairs.

Ruins near Whitfield Lough

I continued through a gateway, up steeply past two rowans and back through a gate in a higher wall. The heather-covered slopes beyond gradually levelled out onto the broad summit, almost a plateau, of Williamston Common. Ahead lay miles of open bog and wide sky, at first glance featureless, perhaps even monotonous, which slid eventually into the valley of the West Allen.

Though these hills are part of the same chain as the Cheviots, they have their own character. Absent are the narrow, intricate valleys, which cut into their northern counterparts. Here the land rises high and stays high, establishing the pattern which prevails through the centre of England as far south as the Peak. The county border, having risen and fallen tortuously from its northern limit, now crawls up past the 500-metre contour, below which it does not dip for something like twenty kilometres. The roads which link the Allen and Tyne valleys are the highest in Northumberland, taking the motorist to greater altitudes than even the highest passes of the Lake District.

Across this land, the wind blows unrestrained, flattening heather and moor grass with its withering gusts. Its moan and hiss are punctuated by the call of buzzard, raven, curlew and golden plover. When white clouds race across the sky, they are often pursued by darker omens, which carry a pitiless drizzle. And while you shiver in this, you can be mocked, at the same time, by a sunny slope not a mile away.

Yet this is all part of the beauty of the North Pennines. Its loneliness frightens some. Its full appreciation may be an acquired taste. But to those who do appreciate it, the scenery is as fine as any in England.

I stepped out across the moor, following the fence. What little track there was had been largely obscured by heather. The valley noises had fallen behind, to be replaced by the squelch of footfall on damp ground, and the sudden whirr and cackle of scattering grouse. Small hollows hid patches of sphagnum bog above which dragonflies darted. Numerous peacock butterflies flew over drier parts of the path.

I stopped for lunch amid limestone boulders, which lay scattered around a peaty hollow at the lowest part of the moor. Across to my right, the monochrome of moor grass was broken only by a dark patch of conifers that peered out of the upper reaches of Barhaugh Burn.

The land rose again steadily. I jumped from tussock to tussock to cross a large area of sodden sphagnum moss. At the top of the rise a quarried hollow sheltered the mortarless walls of a ruined building. Just above this, the ground levelled out before sloping gently down to the shores of Whitfield Lough, the highest natural lake in the county.

The lake was silent, rippled only by the breeze. At times scores of nesting black-headed gulls would populate its surface, and lapwing, curlew, golden plover and meadow pipit would feed around its shores. Today, only a single common gull floated near the far shore.

and eggs of golden plover,
Whitfield Lough

I returned to the fence and followed it to the trig point and stone hut, which marked the summit of Whitfield Moor. Beyond this watershed, the hill sloped down toward the West Allen, which lay about the same distance in front of me as did the South Tyne behind. On the far skyline, the Allendale chimneys, stark reminders of the long-dead lead mining industry, glinted sharply in the sun.

I turned south and followed the fence across an almost level stretch to another small top. The distant view this time was dominated by Cross Fell and Great Dun Fell, the highest peaks in the Pennines.

I dropped more steeply to the sharp gully of Barhaugh Burn. This proved deeper than I anticipated and hid a surprise. The stream from the upper hillside trickled under the fence, across a stone table and cascaded down a stepped crag overhung with rowans. It continued through a short rocky gorge and disappeared into the conifer forest. It was not spectacular, but it was certainly beautiful, and added that small touch of magic which often comes with an unexpected moment near the end of a good day in the hills.

There was little else for me to do now, but climb out of the far side of the gorge and up to the crest of the ridge. From there, I joined a track down toward Barhaugh, picked up the surfaced road and followed it back to Slaggyford.

These modest hills are little over half the height of those of the Lake District, not far to the west. They lack ruggedness and spectacle; only the initial slopes above Slaggyford could be described as steep. Everywhere else is gently undulating. But this is a deceptive wilderness. On the shores of Whitfield Lough, you feel a long way from anywhere, and that a slight accident or change in the weather could leave you very exposed. The essence of the area is in its bleakness, which can be enjoyed by anyone prepared to make a modest effort.

Bird footprints in wet peat, Whitfield Lough

Stephen Goodwin

9 Flat-capped fiend: Cross Fell, North Pennines

'Look at the icicles,' said Lucie. 'Fabulous!' And so they were, a crystal curtain across a band of peat on a flank of Cross Fell. Nature had turned alchemist, so great was the contrast. The term 'peat hag' pretty well sums up the unloveliness of these faces of black earth under a fringe of rank and dripping grasses. But as the droplets, by some magic that seemed to me beyond science, had been plasticised and frozen into hanging tapers and full-depth columns, this ordinary bank was transformed with a sun-catching brilliance unmatched by any palace chandelier.

That's really the story of Cross Fell. It may look a featureless hump from the distance of the M6, when most hill-goers will be focused on the opposite side of the motorway and the eagerly-awaited Lake District hills. But get its rough turf under your boots and there will always be some unexpected fold in the land, an unobtrusive alpine flower or quartering predator to wonder at.

icles, flank of Cross Fell

Of course, I'm biased through a kind of kinship. After a day wrestling with words, the walk from my back door that serves as my usual evening circuit follows the west bank of the River Eden. Across the meadows and farmland on the far side, the heaving line of the Pennines stretches from north to south as far as the eye can see, with the table top of Cross Fell pre-eminent.

Greg's Shop on Cross Fell, one of England's most remote buildings

At 2930 feet (893 m), it is the highest hill in all England outside the Lake District. Some years a line of snow braids its distinctive top until after the swallows have arrived to feed over the river. And often, at any time of year, the summit itself is capped – by Cross Fell's oddly personal cloud. 'Cross Fell's got his hat on,' we'll remark, though I have not adduced any useful piece of weather lore to accompany this phenomenon.

Little Dun Fell and its neighbour, Great Dun with the Ministry of Defence giant golf ball, will be visible on the south side, and Skirwith Fell forming a shoulder on the north. Between will be a veil of cloud, enveloping the mile-wide summit plateau. Just occasionally the 'hat' floats free, appearing as a lenticular flat cap poised above the bare pate of the fell.

Lime kiln above Kir

On that February morning of the icicles, we had set off from Kirkland to walk the 10 miles over to Garrigill in the upper valley of the South Tyne. It is a route of some antiquity. Until the 19th century, Garrigill did not have a church and its dead had to be carried across the spine of England for burial in the consecrated ground of St Lawrence's church at Kirkland. How the people of Garrigill must have longed for their sick loved ones to cling to life until a spell of clement weather.

The Old Corpse Road quickly casts off the confines of moss-clad walls and ash trees beside Kirkland Beck and heads for the open fellside, climbing steadily beneath the broken edge of High Cap, typical of the rocky scars which stand high on the broad ridges extending outwards from the main Pennine chain.

'Open' is the operative word anywhere along the escarpment known to Eden Valley dwellers as the East Fellside. It's not just the huge view back across the valley to Lakeland and north to the Solway and Scotland, but the limitless skyscape and often scouring wind. England's only named wind, the 'Helm', tears down these hillsides in spring and autumn, destroying blossoms and tender plants, yet by some meteorological freak curls on itself, dissipates and never crosses the river.

Always, as the track turns High Cap, my eyes are drawn to the cliffs of Black Doors at the head of wild Ardale. A band of broken dolerite columns and two deeply incised rocky gullies, Black Doors is an outcrop of the Great Whin Sill, that same volcanic sheet that gives us the more dramatic High Cup Nick further south in the Pennines. Cross Fell is a real mix of rock. Most of it is a mix of gritstone and shale, with its resistant cap girdled by scree, while on the Eden flank are limestone scars – with old kilns lower down.

Evidence of the Pennines' mining past is everywhere. There is a disused level just behind my viewpoint of Black Doors. And from the same spot you can see lower down Ardale to where the trace of the Roman road called Maiden Way cuts down the grassy defile of Lad Slack, fords the beck and continues its straight line over to Kirkland. History has been busy below Cross Fell.

Snow covered the scree above Black Doors and we weren't tempted to divert to its deep portals. In summer though this is a place for botany, with plants such as alpine scurvy grass mantling the rocks. The Corpse Road over Skirwith Fell can become truly glutinous, but with the ground frozen, we soon reached the tall cairn of Yad Stone, by the watershed, and descended to the open bothy of Greg's Hut, a stone-built 'cottage' at an abandoned lead mine.

From the Yad Stone to Garrigill, the Corpse Road is also the line of the Pennine Way, so there would be more walkers on warmer days. This eight-mile stretch over the high moors must be a joy for Wayfarers, but for myself, the magic wanes on this side of the hill. This is keepered land, managed for the red grouse, or rather for the benefit of their assailants, and denuded of the hen harriers, buzzards and peregrines that would naturally have a home here. The moor starts to feel sterile and the track, well maintained for the ease of the shooters, gets monotonous.

Better by far to turn uphill at Yad Stone, skirt the screes and head across the plateau to the stony windbreak and trig point on the summit of Cross Fell itself. It's said you can see eight old counties from up here on a clear day. Looking across Eden's patchwork of pasture, wheat and woodland, the Lakeland fells appear in blue-grey profile, alluringly mountainous, yet there is a feeling of satisfaction that I'm here, and not over there.

Perhaps because of the howling Helm, the plateau was believed in the Dark Ages to be the haunt of demons and was called Fiends' Fell until St Augustine banished the evil spirits by erecting a cross and altar on the summit. Both are long gone. Almost anything could be imagined in the mists, but in spring and summer any melancholy note is likely to be the 'tlui' of the golden plover which forage up here.

Heading home, we usually follow a little used track angling below Wildboar Scar – limestone this, with short-cropped turf and tormentil below. The buzzards are back, circling above the gorsy tangles by Littledale Beck.

And before Kirkland, Cross Fell's past has one more offering for us as we walk by the Hanging Walls of Mark Anthony. To the untutored eye these are nowhere near as exotic as the name on the OS map suggests, just hummocks in a field. But they were once cultivation terraces or strip lynchets; shadows in the grass left by pastoralists who knew the flat-capped fell 1600 years before the birth of Christ.

Dun Fell from a cairn high on Cross Fell

Jon Sparks
10 Rock icon:
Dow Crag, Lake District

Kate had climbed several times, but only on indoor walls and small outcrops. We thought she was ready for the real thing, and there could be no better introduction than Dow Crag.

We pointed it out from the top of Trowbarrow Quarry, a triangle of shadows vague in the distance, and we tried to tell her why we loved it so much: it was a crag for everyone, where easy climbs cross paths with desperate Extremes; a wild place, yet easy to reach; a crag which is also a fell, where climbs end close to a summit.

Climbers on Eliminate A

But words can only take you so far. She would have to experience it.

Summit of Dow Crag, looking to Scafell and Scafell Pike

On the day she was at our door early, eager yet nervous, talking too much, hopping about as we finished packing. In the car she chattered on until we crested the little ridge between Coniston Water and Torver and the crag swaggered into view, near and solid and massive. She didn't say another word until we had parked on the edge of the village, shouldered sacks and set out.

We climbed through spring-bright woods and out onto open fell. The crag kept disappearing and reappearing as we crossed dips and rises before the final rocky pull to Goat's Water. We skirted the dark tarn, plodded up the scree, sunlit buttresses and shadow-flooded gullies hanging over us.

At the foot of the crag there's an old blue stretcher box, which made Kate shudder, but I pointed out that it hadn't seen much use lately. We worked up diagonally left, pausing to watch a leader picking her way up Leopard's Crawl, moving with precision on holds invisible to us.

Finally we scrambled into the mouth of Great Gully, where Giant's Crawl starts. It's graded 'Difficult', which in the paradoxical language of climbing grades means it's easy. Kate knew this; she'd climbed Diffs aplenty on smaller crags. But it was cold below the gloomy gully, the rock slippery and awkward, and I was slow to get going, fiddling with gear and creeping upwards in fits and starts. Watching intently, Kate's upturned face was white and tense.

I pulled onto a broad slab that had been soaking up the sun for several hours. As its warmth seeped into my limbs I finally began to move with some fluency. Bernie then demonstrated how the pitch should be climbed, and soon it was Kate's turn. A brief hesitation, then she pressed her lips together and committed herself. The supple impetuosity of youth made light of the awkward section. She came steadily up the slab, a grin spreading as she too felt the warmth of the rock.

On Tiger Traverse

While Bernie made steady progress up the next pitch, we watched a climber working up steep walls beyond the gully. I identified the route as Eliminate A, a middle-grade classic to which Kate could aspire.

My turn came, leaving her alone on the ledge as I climbed out of sight. The second pitch climbs a narrow ribbon of rock, with nothing but steep rock above and emptiness below. The climbing is easy enough, the age-old rock solid as steel, but the sense of isolation is palpable. I wondered how Kate would cope.

The rope came in with encouraging speed, and the moment she saw us she started to relate how a climber had appeared from below, as if out of nowhere. She was fired up now, agog to see where the route went next. After a slight break where lush ledges sprout unexpected bluebells, it soon gets serious again, veering left and rising to a protruding block on the skyline.

From the ledge just beyond the block, we couldn't see Kate, but we could hear her scuffling and gasping. The rope had stopped coming in. Bernie lengthened her belay and leaned out to see better, then offered a few quiet words. Like so many before, Kate had wriggled too deeply into the crack beside the block; it took a little persuasion to get her to back down slightly, then lean out to find good holds on the block. A swing and a kick and she was with us on the ledge, breathlessly apologising. But we both remembered how hard it can be to launch out of a sheltered crack; everyone says it's like leaving the womb.

Once she was tied on, we invited her to admire the exposure; from the edge by her toes the next stop was the scree a hundred metres below. Her eyes went wide for a moment, but then she shook herself and grinned. Fear is the spice of climbing.

Looking up at A Buttress, with Easy Gully (L) and Great Gully (R)

From this point the route goes straight up, on huge warm holds. Soon the rock begins to lie back, and then there's a level grassy crest, a little island in the sky, with deep gullies either side.

We all flopped onto the ground. I pulled off my tight rock-shoes, let my toes luxuriate in the cool grass. The world beyond the climb came back into focus: tiny figures across the gulf on on the ridge of the Old Man; climbers' calls and the chime of karabiners floating up from below; a raven drifting past, sparing us a glance before shooting off with the merest shrug of a wing.

We lounged there, feasting on lukewarm water and flapjack. As Kate observed, it tasted great. Then we packed up and changed into walking boots. The weight of the sacks seemed shocking; it always does. The gear feels a lot lighter when you're using it. And it's a small price to pay.

We crossed the narrow neck leading to the main ridge of the fell. The summit, a bristle of rocks, was a couple of minutes away, and it was deserted; a rare privilege. The air was still, the silence hinting at things we couldn't quite hear.

The fells ranged away northward, flat and translucent in the soft haze, slightly translucent, like photographs of themselves held up to light. The Isle of Man was a smudge on the western horizon. To the south, Morecambe Bay lay shimmering in the sun beyond rumpled lowlands and the long blue strip of Coniston Water.

We wondered about another climb, but Kate declared Giant's Crawl was enough for one day, if we didn't mind. We were perfectly happy to saunter down the ridge, over the minor rises of Buck Pike and Brown Pike, to the Walna Scar track. Back at the bridge just before the turnoff for Torver, we paused to look back at the crag. Wrapping itself in shadows now, it looked bigger, colder and steeper.

Kate gazed for a minute, gave herself a little shake as if she couldn't believe she'd been up there, then turned to us with a huge grin. 'Y'know what?' she said. 'Dow Crag rocks'.

Dow Crag from Goat's Water with dark gashes Easy Gully (L) and Great Gully (R) defining A Buttress

Robert Swain

11 The wet Sahara: Morecambe Bay

I see Morecambe Bay, often touching on it at some point, nearly every day when I am out walking my dog. When I don't see it, it is covered in mist or haze.

The Bay has many moods, affected by the tides, the weather and the season. I have been on it when the weather was so hot that it was the only place to get a breath of air. But I have also known it covered with ice floes. I have been at Heysham Head when the wind was so strong I could not stand up and had to retreat to the local pub. At the time of writing it is in a benign mood, but a year earlier it made national news when twenty-one cocklers lost their lives when they were cut off by the advancing tide.

Morecambe Bay stretches round from near Fleetwood in Lancashire to Barrow-in-Furness in Cumbria, and is the second largest estuarial bay in England. This vast expanse of sand and mud with river channels flowing through it is covered by fast-flowing tides twice a day. It has been dubbed Britain's 'wet Sahara'.

Sunset, Morecambe Bay

Over the years many lives have been lost out on the Bay, which is why there is a Queen's Guide to escort travellers across it. This essential post has been in existence since at least 1501, when the Prior of Cartmel paid for the first official guide across the Kent Sands to Hest Bank.

The present guide is Cedric Robinson, well-known to the many thousands of people he has escorted from either Hest Bank or Arnside to Kents Bank, close to Grange-over-Sands. Before taking a party over the Sands, Cedric goes out on the same tide the day before to mark out the route with 'brobs', traditionally sprigs of laurel. On the day I crossed, as always, he prodded the sands before finally deciding on the point at which to lead us across the channel of the River Kent.

The courses of the rivers are constantly changing; the Kent is sometimes close in to the Grange shore, but at other times across towards Arnside. The route followed by Cedric is never straight, as there is the constant danger of treacherous quicksands. While it looks only a comparatively short distance across from Arnside to Grange, for part of the time my party was walking towards Bolton-le-Sands before crossing the river.

The tides and the river channels move about vast quantities of sand. In July 2004 the River Keer, which enters the Bay at Carnforth, drastically changed its channel by moving close in to the Hest Bank shore. Local people were surprised to see the old Hest Bank pier reappear after it had been covered by sand and not seen in living memory. The river washed away the sand to reveal a substantial stone structure about nine feet high, which people must have been walking over for years without knowing what lay beneath their feet.

Windblown hawthorn, Humphrey Head

Pattern of channels in Morecambe Bay from Arnside Knott

Silverdale has lost its foreshore in recent years. Previously a person was able to ride out on horseback over grass far enough to see Arnside. I recently had to take care walking along the head of the shore near The Cove where I had, in the past, walked on grass. Off Jenny Brown's Point, the stones of an old reclamation scheme are now well exposed, having been under sand, and it would no longer be possible for a coach to leave the Sands and go up Cow's Mouth to the road into Silverdale.

Arnside is the point at which many people watch the bore coming up the Bay – travelling faster than a galloping horse. One of my earliest recollections of the Bay is of the bore sweeping around at Arnside, the water rapidly covering what had been dry ground only minutes earlier.

Further round the Bay at Grange-over-Sands the story is very different. Old photographs by the former Clare House Pier, a structure that is long gone, show that the beach shelved much more steeply before being silted up. Now, grass has grown and what has become a saltmarsh extends over a considerable area. Sheep now graze where boats once sailed.

The flocks of birds that visit the Bay find it a vast feeding ground which has been likened to their equivalent of a Mars Bar. Waders such as knot, dunlin, redshank, bar-tailed godwit, oystercatcher and curlew, feed in the sand and mud while gulls sail on the tide or fly overhead. In winter at Grange-over-Sands I have had black-headed gulls feed from my hand. Ducks and geese such as shelduck, wigeon, and greylag geese are seen regularly, depending on the season.

Stretching from the edge of the shore below near Warton Crag to about two miles inland is the Leighton Moss RSPB Reserve, a haven for bird watchers from its several hides. Many species of birds are to be seen depending on the season. I have never spotted the elusive bittern among the swaying reeds, but I have heard its foghorn boom in spring.

The limestone country around the Bay provides excellent walking and the opportunity to study the unique flora and fauna. A wander up Hampsfell above Grange-over-Sands to the Hospice takes you over the clints and grikes of limestone pavement. There are excellent views around the Bay from the fell. More limestone walking is to be found on Warton Crag, around the Silverdale and Arnside Area of Outstanding Beauty, on Whitbarrow, and around the Furness Peninsula.

Humphrey Head is another nature reserve jutting out into the Bay near Kents Bank, its western side a natural limestone cliff. In 1677, much of the Bolton-le-Sands saltmarsh was carried across the Bay by the River Kent and deposited here, covering 100 acres of land, according to the autobiography of Lancaster merchant William Stout. There is also the story that the last wolf in England was killed near Humphrey Head, sometime in the 14th century.

Over the years there have been various land reclamation schemes around the Bay. In particular, much land was claimed from the sea following the building of the railway line from Ulverston to Lancaster, which opened in 1857. There have been various other schemes: to dam the Bay and have a railway line or a road running on its top; to build large water storage reservoirs in the Bay; and to reclaim much larger areas of land.

But I wonder how anybody could want to try to control this fascinating area – and whether Morecambe Bay would ultimately let them.

Morecambe Bay (watercolour by David Bellamy)

Tom Waghorn

12 Crags and crashes: Bleaklow, Peak District

'You're fired!' Gamekeeper Joe Townsend was furious … not a single grouse had been shot on the drive. He paid me the full daily beaters' wage of 10 shillings (50p) and grudgingly organised a lift back to Glossop for me down the Snake Pass.

As a hillwalker and naturalist, I adore the red grouse. I love to see them leap into the air on spreading wings and descend steeply, extending their necks and feet and fanning their tails. Above all, I cherish their barking call: 'Go-back, go bak-bak-bak-bak-bak'.

Nearly 60 years ago, I was less enlightened. As a fifth-former at Glossop Grammar School, I was hired in the summer holidays as a beater on the Peakland moors. A line of beaters, waving white flags on six foot sticks, drove the grouse towards the shooting butts … and to eternity.

Moorland wilderness between Higher Shelf Stones and Bleaklow Head

Higher Shelf Stones seen ne[ar] summit of Snake Pass

Walker crossing moorland

Many of the poor creatures were only winged by the hail of leadshot. And I'll never forget the horror of seeing them lying, still alive, among the heather and watching my fellow beaters pick them up by their feet and bang the birds' heads on their boots to dispatch them.

It was a typically misty day, about 1800 feet up on Bleaklow. We were to do two drives in the morning and three in the afternoon. The butts were arranged back-to-back and after one sweep, the beaters would swing round and drive the grouse back to the second set of butts. Two of us became lost and separated from the main party of beaters. When the grouse saw us, they did a clumsy U-turn and flew back over the waving flags.

I wasn't too worried about being sacked. Bleaklow has always been my favourite wilderness. In a largely synthetic world, we long for wildness, for what seems untouched. And I resented seeing so many people defiling those magical acres of heather, bilberry, cloudberry, cotton grass and above all the cloying peat, which has the consistency of thick, black porridge.

Bleaklow has been described as 'Britain's only true desert'. Maybe that's overstating it: at 2077 feet (633 m) Bleaklow Head barely nudges over the 2000-ft contour required for mountainhood. But parts of this moorland offer an exquisite sense of remoteness – I'm thinking of Grinah Stones, Grains in the Water, the Upper Alport or the Upper Westend valleys.

*   *   *

I have one other abiding schooldays memory of Bleaklow. On November 3 1948, Captain Landon P Tanner had dropped the nose of his giant B-29 Superfortress through the clouds to check his position … and ploughed into Shelf Moor above the Snake Pass.

All thirteen American crew members died as flames engulfed the shattered aircraft. Their bodies were found by members of the RAF Mountain Rescue Service who had climbed onto the mist-shrouded moor.

It was the time of the Berlin airlift, when photographic reconnaissance planes like the B-29 were used to spy on the Russians. But the four-engined Superfortress – ironically named Over Exposed, the same type of plane used to drop the atomic bombs over Hiroshima and Nagasaki – was on a routine flight from RAF Scampton in Lincolnshire to Burtonwood, near Warrington, when it crashed.

I remember the bodies being brought down by stretcher to the top of the Snake Pass, and the rumour sweeping Glossop that the Burtonwood payroll was lost on Bleaklow.

A day or so later, a small group of us boys combed the moor, looking for the payroll. We didn't find it, of course – the bag containing the $7000 had been quickly recovered. But I do remember picking up a heavy aerial camera and humping it down the Doctor's Gate track to Glossop.

With all the brashness of youth, I took it into Glossop Grammar School next day. The physics master was less than pleased, and I was instructed to return it. I walked the six miles back to the wreckage and buried the camera nearby.

Ever since, the wreckage has been a place of pilgrimage for me. For some weeks after the crash, the tailplane reared 20 feet into the air like a giant finger of fate. A rescue Jeep had been abandoned in Devil's Dike below the site, and it lay there, rusting and forgotten, for years.

An American demolition team eventually blew up the bigger sections of the wreck. But much of it is still there today, scattered over 200 square yards of peaty moorland just to the east of the trig point at Higher Shelf Stones. Four engines, part of a wing and the landing-wheels are morbid reminders of that fateful November day. You can still pick up chunks of scattered metal and, surprisingly, some of the aluminium is just as shiny bright as when it was made.

Superfortress wreckage near Higher Shelf Stones

Thousands of ramblers and a few aircraft archaeologists visit the site. There's a small memorial plaque and wooden crosses and poppies are placed reverently near the wreckage. When I was last there, someone had re-created the shape of the giant plane in stones on the peat.

Everyone who goes there reflects on one simple point. Another 50 feet or so higher and Over Exposed would have skimmed clear of the ground and completed its journey safely. And the final irony was that the crew had just finished their tour of service overseas, and were due to fly home to the States in just three days' time.

The B-29 wreckage is one of a number of wrecks in the Bleaklow area. It is illegal to do any digging or remove any pieces of the aircraft without first getting permission from the Ministry of Defence and the landowner. But, over the years, souvenir hunters have plundered most of the sites.

* * *

From crashes to crags. The late Eric Byne, in his superbly-researched *High Peak* of 1966, commented that Bleaklow was 'so vast that the crags tend to get lost in in the background'.

Nevertheless, there's splendid gritstone climbing at Shining Clough (mentioned in Shelagh Delaney's play, *A Taste of Honey*) and at Yellowslacks (once famously and unsuccessfully dynamited by the farmer at Mossy Lea in a futile bid to stop climbers).

Outdoor types have a unique affection for Bleaklow, just as for Kinder Scout. The ashes of access campaigner Benny Rothman were scattered there. So were those of fellow Mass Trespasser, folk singer and dramatist, Ewan MacColl (whose real name was Jimmy Miller, from Salford). No doubt members of his family were recalling the words from his 1986 ballad, The Joy of Living:

> *Take me to some high place of heather, rock and ling,*
> *Scatter my dust and ashes, feed me to the wind.*
> *So that I will be a part of all you see, the air you are breathing.*

The 'Kissing Stones', Wain Stones, Bleaklow Head

Chris Craggs

13 Throne of the gods: Stanage Edge, Peak District

It is well over half a lifetime ago but I remember it well, my first inspirational sight of Stanage Edge – the Throne of the Gritstone Gods, as Walt Unsworth so accurately described it in his book *The English Outcrops*.

After a journey down from North Yorkshire in the back of a van, and a cold, near sleepless night camped at North Lees, I was up early. The view was breathtaking, a hard black line, backlit against the eastern sky, stretched from horizon to horizon. A callow youth gazed in awe at the ribbon of rock which disappeared in both directions. It looked like the crag would hold enough adventures to last a lifetime.

Fast forward thirty five years, and he is still there, tramping the crest of the edge in bitter weather, and exploring every facet of this special place on kinder days. I have got to know Stanage pretty well by now, having written a couple of climbing guidebooks and, over the years since that first encounter, there have been adventures aplenty and heaps of great memories. Despite this intimacy with the place, odd surprises still turn up, and even though I have spent the intervening three and a half decades climbing all over Europe and the United States, it is still a venue I hold in the highest esteem.

North-west across The Plantation to the distant High Neb, Stanage

The first spring evening on the rock is always a special time, like meeting old friends, with half a dozen classics ticked-off and a retreat to quiet corner of a pub to compare scars (the rock is very abrasive) and make plans both near and far.

The gritstone edges of the Peak District have a presence in climbing mythology far greater than their diminutive stature might suggest. They are surrounded by the industrial cities of the North and Midlands and have been used as an escape route from the drudgery of city life for well over 100 years. The names of the first ascensionists is almost a roll-call of the great and good in British climbing: Puttrell, Berg, Harding, Brown, Whillans and Fawcett – and new names are constantly being added to the list.

Grades, techniques and equipment have always been pushed to the limit, and it wouldn't be far from the truth to say that every decent climber that the country has produced cut their teeth on these rough outcrops, and that the skills learned here have served them well in more far-flung arenas.

Stanage Edge is composed millstone grit, a dark compact rock which is a climbing medium par excellence. Its even texture and peerless friction made it the ideal material for the artefact which gave the rock its name, and the millstone became the symbol of the Peak District National Park – the first in Britain.

High Neb Buttress on a perfect summer's day

Footpath through The Plantation approaching Stanage Edge

There are now over a thousand named climbs routes on Stanage, from short amiable scrambles to some of the hardest outings anywhere in the world. Although only attaining a maximum height of 20 metres (65ft), the steepness and solidity of the rock means that the climbs often feel harder than their grade would suggest. Modern equipment has developed to such an extent that few of the climbs are the serious undertakings that they once were, though despite this, accidents do still happen.

Over recent years Stanage's reputation has spread and it has become incredibly popular, with teams turning up from all over the UK on fine summer weekends, and the names of the best-known climbs cropping up in conversations anywhere in the world where climbers meet.

The original Victorian pioneers in their tweeds and heavily-nailed boots would doubtless be shocked by the number of visitors and awed by the modern climber's abilities. With sticky-soled shoes, nylon ropes, sophisticated hardware and gymnast's chalk, equipment has changed radically, though the thrill of pulling onto the cliff top after making a successful ascent hasn't diminished down the years. To me, visits to Stanage have become more about having a pleasant time with friends and doing classic climbs in a great setting than, as in the old days, about daring deeds and pushing oneself to the limit.

Soloing one of Stanage's 1000 routes

The crag turns its back on Sheffield, the industrial city where so many of its devotees live, and faces west towards the setting sun. Evenings spent climbing on the cliff are special times. The drudgery of the nine-to-five existence are left behind and a few hours of freedom, watching the sun finally slide behind the Pennines, is a good a way to achieve closure before heading down the hill and back to reality.

Early visitors to the crag were generally transients, travellers and traders cutting across the high and wild moors as quickly as possible. The Long Causeway, which slices through the centre of the crag, is the best example of one of their routes, linking the Cheshire plain west of the Pennines to the industrial centres to the east. The men who quarried and shaped the millstones were probably the first people to spend much time up here, and it would be interesting to know what they thought of the setting as they crafted away. On warm days, there could have been fewer finer workshops, though winters up here must have been especially grim.

Like everywhere else in our crowded islands, Stanage suffers from pressures. What with grouse shooting, off-road vehicles, hang-gliders, nesting birds, sheep-rearing, ramblers and of course, the ever-increasing number of climbers, the demands on it are considerable. Fortunately, due to common sense and a bit of consideration, conflicts have been few and far between.

I have driven past the crag on damp days when the place was cloaked in clinging low cloud and late on in the gathering gloom of summer evenings after climbing elsewhere in the Peak, and there is almost always a car or two in the car park, such is the attraction of the place.

Maybe I'm getting a little selfish as the years roll by, but I prefer to visit Stanage on quieter days now, midweek or out of season, or even when the weather is less than perfect. That way I am more likely to have the place to myself. Despite that, if you are up there on a quiet day and see an older chap gazing wistfully out from the crag with a faraway look in his eyes, please say hello. It might be me.

Sunset from Stanage Edge

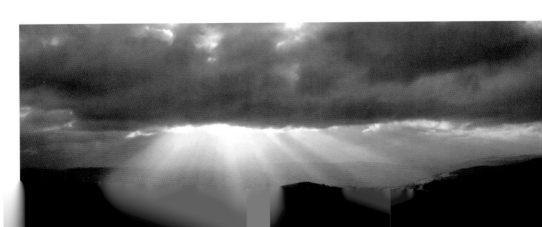

Andrew McCloy
14 Making sense of it all: Arbor Low, Peak District

There are occasional moments in my life when I feel I am on the verge of an incredibly profound thought. It's as if I am hovering around some magic portal and am about to be transported to a place of infinite knowledge and understanding, revealing why we're all here and how everything connects.

I had such an experience at the prehistoric stone circle of Arbor Low, in the Derbyshire White Peak, a few years ago. Sitting quite alone on top of the encircling grassy ramparts, I was staring out across the hills in an unfocused fashion, when suddenly it all made sense. Or, at least, it very nearly did. Unfortunately, as soon as I sprung into conscious deliberation the moment was lost, and a few minutes later I was wandering down the road thinking of dinner.

Looking west from Arbor Low

But this strange, wild place made a lasting impression on me, and I've been back many times to immerse myself in the landscape and soak up the atmosphere of a location that has evidently has been special for others, for whatever reason, over at least five thousand years.

Let me describe both the monument and the place, since they are equally important. The setting, in itself, is not especially dramatic. A mile south of the village of Monyash in the centre of the so-called White Peak, the stone circle sits on the top of a low, rounded hill, a short walk from the lane. The approach is through a small livestock farm, with a patchwork quilt of grazing fields divided by traditional drystone walls beyond.

It's when you reach the top, and stand at the entrance to the henge that the location hits you. I've watched people bound up to the stones, chattering excitedly as the circle is revealed from behind the banks, and then a few moments later turn round and gaze, as if rather taken aback, at the unfolding spectacle.

It's not that it's an inherently beautiful, nor even conventionally dramatic, view – there are no soaring peaks or plunging dales. Instead, at your feet, lies a broad limestone plateau, a bare and green vastness that extends for miles to the east, north and west. Monyash, the only proper settlement, is hidden in a dip in the centre, and so it is a curiously featureless landscape that entices the eye to pick out the odd clump of woodland here or an isolated farmstead there.

It's an unusual view and I would imagine a little perplexing for those who think of the Peak District solely in terms of narrow limestone dales or lofty heather moors. This is not exactly picture postcard stuff, and perhaps is all the better for it.

Massive recumbent stone, Arbor Low

Looking towards Gib Hill (right) at sunrise

However, the other ingredient that makes this location special, and contributes to a palpable sense of wildness, is its altitude. Arbor Low sits astride a 1200-foot ridge, which accounts for the far-reaching views, the incredible sense of space and light, and also the keen wind that can, at times, make standing upright difficult. Best to contemplate one's navel sitting down here, I find.

And so to the monument itself. It consists of a massive earth bank or henge, around 250 feet in diameter, which encloses a large circle of around 50 stones in various states of recumbency. Many of the limestone slabs are wonderfully weathered, cracked and pock-marked, and laid out flat like a game of Neolithic clock patience, with the king stone in the middle. Experts generally agree that the stones once stood upright, but why, when and how is anyone's guess.

The henge monument dates from around 2,500 BC, but was it primarily a meeting place or trading point, or did it have some sort of ceremonial function? Excavations have revealed human bones and various tools and arrowheads; and to the south is a faint bank that leads towards the remains of Gib Hill barrow, where human cremations from 3,000 BC have been discovered.

Arbor Low (from the Old English *Eorthburg Hlaw* or the earthwork hill) remains a special place because it is off the beaten track. Beyond the modest car park there are few signs or prohibitive notices, and instead of interpretation boards telling you what to think you are encouraged to approach the henge with your mind clear and senses alert. You can even touch the stones, climb on them, hug them. It couldn't be farther removed from Stonehenge …

With the exception of the solstices, which attract the usual weird crowd, there never seems to be many people at the stones, and often I have them to myself. Arbor Low is a place that you have to search out, and walk through a farmyard and fields to reach; and with no café or gift shop, there's little to draw the casual visitor.

I have sat by the stones in the fresh morning sunshine with the skylarks trilling furiously overhead and found the sense of peace overwhelming; but it is equally moving to stand beside the stones and feel the gathering evening gloom drawing in and the sky power down for the day. I've also ventured up there in the dead of night, for with a clear sky and an absence of artificial light, this is surely the best natural planetarium in the whole of Derbyshire.

The profundity that I sometimes feel when I'm at the stone circle is not unique to Arbor Low. Some mountains have a similar effect on me; but there are none that I can walk to from my door. Besides, I can't pencil in a diary date for spiritual cleansing every time I go north to the Lakes or the Scottish Highlands. The call of the wild is, by definition, an ungovernable and mysterious thing.

I go to Arbor Low not so much to escape the modern world or to search out some lost wilderness, nor simply to revel in its physical beauty, but because it seems to help to clear my sometimes cluttered mind. The wide-ranging views, the landscape and the sense of space and peace; the mystery of the stones and the immense historical connections embodied in this enigmatic ancient monument: I let my mind drift into neutral and absorb all of this.

And just occasionally, it almost makes some kind of sense.

Arbor Low at sunset

John Cleare

15 Wessex heights: Hambledon and Hod Hills, Dorset

There are some heights in Wessex,
Shaped as if by kindly hand
For thinking, dreaming, dying on…
from *Wessex Heights* by Thomas Hardy

It snowed. For ten days it snowed and life in the small ice-encrusted tent in Everest's Western Cwm became a progression in misery. Excellent tent-mate though he was, my American companion was no match for Thomas Hardy. Tears flowed as I followed Tess's evocative wanderings through green Dorset, around the verdant Blackmore Vale and over wind-swept Cranborne Chase. Hardy is heavy going at the best of times, but dreams of spring in England – in Wessex – still held the Himalayan blizzard at bay.

Fast forward fifteen years and I found myself living on the fringe of Cranborne Chase. It was there to explore, and I'd invested in the appropriate twenty-five thou' maps even before we'd moved. With its steep downland scarps and deep, hidden coombs, crisscrossed with ancient trackways and drove roads, scattered with small, secluded villages and steeped in history – it was not 'de-forested' as a hunting preserve until 1830 – the Chase more than lived up to my long-harboured expectations.

ikers traverse the ramparts
Hambledon Hill

Obviously my first objective was its highest point, Win Green, a worthy, tree-clump-topped down from which the Needles and the Quantocks were visible on opposite horizons. On the map, however, a heavily-hachured knot of tight contours standing proud from the western escarpment demanded investigation; and thus I discovered the twin hills of Hambledon and Hod.

The chalk escarpments of the Chase and the Dorset Downs enclose Blackmore Vale to the east and south. Between them, through a narrow gap, flows the River Stour, first to Blandford then winding on towards the sea. Commanding the gap stand Hod and Hambledon Hills, the former rearing sheer above the river, the latter jutting into the Vale like the bow of a great ship.

Indeed, many a real mountain might envy Hambledon its dramatic situation and shape, for an Iron Age fortress occupies its narrow prow, guarded by three rows of still-mighty ditched ramparts, well over a mile around, from which slopes of precipitous grass fall over 300 feet – though it could well be a thousand – to the village of Child Okeford and the spreading Vale beyond.

From any direction the ascent is strenuous, but it earns instant reward. The summer breeze ripples the long grass on the ringed ramparts, ox-eye daisies and cowslips scatter the hollow banks while lark song fills the air. Hardy's Vale of the Little Dairies stretches out below into the blue haze of distant Somerset. But Hambledon is wide open to the south-westerlies and in winter, the clouds scud low over the bleached and flattened grass and the Vale is all but invisible in the murk. Sometimes the wind carries the clash of steel and the cries of conflict, for it was here that the Dorset Clubmen made their brave but ultimately futile last stand.

Late summer on the eastern slopes of Hambledon Hill

Orchid on the slopes of Hambledon Hill

Sixteen centuries after the hill fort was abandoned, Civil War rent the country. In 1645, angered by the rampaging and destructive armies of both sides in a quarrel which they felt was not theirs, a group of some 5000 embittered peasants armed themselves with scythes, pitchforks and clubs and, led by a local vicar, rose up against both King and Parliament.

With white cockades in their hats and marching to the cry: 'If you offer to Plunder or take our Cattle, Be assured we'll give you Battle', they assembled on Clubmen's Down on the western scarp of Cranborne Chase. After baiting a Parliamentary patrol at Sturminster Newton and being driven off from Shaftesbury, they retreated behind the ramparts of Hambledon Hill, resolving to fight to the death.

Cromwell was not amused and despatched a troop of dragoons to sort out the Clubmen. This they did with little problem, killing several, wounding many and capturing around 300, though many escaped by sliding down the steep slopes where the horsemen were unable to follow. The prisoners – '… these poor silly creatures' Cromwell called them – were locked up overnight and sent home having been severely warned to behave themselves. Though a mere skirmish, the Clubman's Revolt colours the atmosphere of Hambledon Hill while earlier history can only be left to the imagination.

Hedgerow and wild flowers below Hambledon Hill

A narrow neck links the hill fort to the main mass of Hambledon, where traces of a Neolithic causewayed camp circa 3000 BC surrounds the OS trig point at 630 feet (192 m). Two long barrows stand nearby and excavations here have hinted at human sacrifice. A gradual descent through cornfields leads past a keeper's cottage and down to a lane in a wooded defile at the foot of Hod Hill.

Though this ascent is rather shorter, the grassy slopes are steep and lead directly to the double rampart and fosse that encircle the plateau-like summit, a second and very different Iron Age hill fort. The vaguely rectangular enclosure covers almost forty acres (16 hectares) and an incongruously orderly arrangement of lesser mounds and ditches occupies its highest quadrant. Uniquely, this is a Roman military camp superimposed on a British hill fort.

Not surprisingly, archeologists have been busy on Hod Hill, which seems to have been more of a fortified township than a warriors' stronghold. Apparently there were some 270 dwellings within the ramparts before Vespasian's conquering legions swept through Wessex and laid siege to the settlement in AD 44.

No evidence of serious fighting was found, but ballista bolts lying among the hut circles suggest the place was reduced by an artillery bombardment and the Britons capitulated to avoid unnecessary bloodshed – unlike the bloody battle which took place at Maiden Castle scarcely 20 miles distant. To seal their authority on the area and to command the strategic Stour Gap, the occupying troops built their own fort within the British ramparts. That the Roman fort itself was apparently destroyed by fire a few years later adds a further intriguing twist to the tale.

As I lingered on the orchid-scattered ramparts one summer evening, gazing over the winding Stour at the curling wave of the Downs, I wondered if perhaps the Roman stockade had been assaulted by tribal freedom fighters, striking out from a secret lair in the tangled forests of Cranborne Chase? I like to think so.

Southern portal of the hill fort, Hod Hill

16 *Deer paths to delight: Ashdown Forest, Sussex*

Winter's bracken has been layered down the ever-steepening slope like a series of bronzed roofing tiles, frosted in patches where the weak February sun is unable to penetrate tree or fog, but smooth and glossy where rain doused it a day or so ago. Through it, deer prints cut a path which does not falter; straight down the slope they go, decisive and unwavering, seducing me into a part of the Forest's hinterland, vaguely remembered from past wanderings.

At the foot of the slope, where a stream has over the centuries scoured a mini-canyon through the sand and clay bed, the prints are more numerous. A gathering place, perhaps? They come from left and right; they muddy the bank and confuse my onward journey. But then, my journey has no firm direction; I have no set plan, for as is so often the case, I am drawn here simply to absorb once more the mysteries and the magic of this wild expanse of heath and woodland, inexplicably described by William Cobbett in his eminently-readable Rural Rides, as 'the most villainously ugly spot I ever saw in England'. Villainously ugly?

Reflections in standing water, Ashdown Forest

Almost 200 years after Cobbett, a more sympathetic eye lights on a great windblown stretch of gorse and heather broken here and there by stand of pine, or self-seeded row of birch, whitebeam, hazel or holly. Unfarmed, barely inhabited, with big panoramic views, sunken ghylls and more than enough trails, tracks and rides not recognised by the Ordnance Survey to make it a wonderland in which to get hopelessly lost, Ashdown Forest has a wild form of beauty the more remarkable in that it lies at the heart of what some mistakenly call the overcrowded south-east of England.

On some of its treeless uplands you can gaze north to see beyond the greensand hills the distant line of the North Downs maybe 20 miles away. Then make a 180-degree turn to discover the South Downs as a blue rumpled horizon a similar distance across the Sussex Weald. To east and west the Forest drains into small irregular field patterns, broken with hedgerow and woodland shaw, which characterise this tranquil county of hills and trim villages. And in that vast panorama a dozen shades of green are doused in summer with purple, or the gold of dwarf gorse, or the more prolific wild common gorse where the stonechat perches to chitter in the morning.

There's nightjar and Dartford warbler, skylark and meadow pipit, and the breathless rush of a hen harrier in courting mood, somersaulting and swooping with closed wings above the open spaces where the fallow, roe and muntjac deer forage. Vibrant spaces, they also attract more than a million visitors each year, yet still it's possible to celebrate a sense of remoteness, and sit for an hour alone with wild nature with no one to disturb its essential peace.

Ellison's Pond, Ashdown Fo

Nutley Mill, Ashdown

There are more open spaces than woodland on Ashdown Forest today, for instead of acres of crowding trees, 'forest' refers here to its former status as a royal hunting ground. In the late 13th century it was surrounded by an extensive ditch and fenced bank known as a 'pale' which allowed deer in but effectively prevented them from leaving. Some 300 years later, the 'fforest of Ashdowne' was said to 'containe by admeasurement 13391 acres and 27 perches' – about 5420 hectares.

It's been fought over, mined and exploited. It's been ravaged by fire and battered by storm. In the 15th century, it was the crucible of England's original Black Country after the first iron smelting blast furnace was built in the forest at Newbridge. But iron ore had been extracted from the Weald since pre-Roman times, and the industry had reached such a peak in the 16th century that William Camden was able to describe the region as being 'full of iron mines in sundry places, where for the making and firing whereof there bee furnaces on every side, and a huge deale of wood is yearely spent…'

All that has gone now, save for its memories. While streams continue to flow iron-stained through deep ghylls of moss and harts-tongue fern, and cinder and slag can still be found in various places, Ashdown Forest has returned to a state of wild glory. Its bogs and seepage lines provide a rich habitat for asphodel, cottongrass, carnivorous sundew, and liverwort. But best of all is the marsh gentian whose brilliant blue trumpets can be seen from July to October. These, and so many other plants, feed and enrich the senses, add to the kaleidoscope of colours which paint the forest scene, and attract insects to them – as do the few scooped pools which reflect the light and punctuate the expanse of open heathland.

You can wander for days in any and every direction and experience something akin to remoteness. There is no wilderness, yet it's unquestionably wild and seemingly untamed despite being managed by the Conservators and Forest Rangers, the former whose duty it is to 'regulate and manage the Forest as an amenity … and to conserve it as a quiet and natural area of outstanding beauty'. Despite Cobbett, that it surely is.

Not 40 miles from Central London, on the uppermost crown of the High Weald Area of Outstanding Natural Beauty (AONB), Ashdown Forest has its own unique kind of beauty. And in every season and in every mood of weather I have been tempted there for physical exercise or spiritual refreshment.

So it is that on this February morning I stand among the deer prints beside the rust-coloured stream, and without any conscious decision making, turn right and follow the bank downstream where a woodpecker rattles a dead trunk a hundred paces away. The stream chunters and sprays over lumps of sandstone, then gathers in scum-topped pools where natural dams form. There's a dead tree lying prone from one bank to the other. I clamber onto its back and teeter across, then turn upstream for no obvious reason, and half an hour later find myself drawn into thinning fog through which the sun meekly bleeds.

Here I wander in a world of my own, ignoring all trails until once more the line of a deer's migration takes me off at an angle. Cutting through the bracken, I don't care where it leads me. Just being here is enough.

Ashdown Forest near Friends Clump

Clive Tully

17 *Man-made wilderness: Norfolk and Suffolk Broads*

It sounded for all the world as though someone was lurking in the reeds, puffing across the neck of a large earthenware pot like a demented refugee from a jug band. Hollow, deep, and penetrating – the sound was almost like a foghorn.

The air was warm and still as I plodded along the Weaver's Way just south of Hickling Broad, and I knew the sound emanating from the reed bed could be only one thing. Once, the heron-like bird in question was so numerous it was shot in large numbers for Victorian dinner tables. It's a different story now, with only around 20 breeding pairs in the whole country, and I knew just how lucky I was with my first encounter with the elusive bittern.

Traditional pleasure wherry White Moth on the River Bure

St Benet's Abbey, near Lu[...]

Rewind a number of years, and my first encounter with the Norfolk and Suffolk Broads came as rather more of a shock. Driving along the Acle straight towards Great Yarmouth, I suddenly became aware of a sail, drifting surreally across the fields to one side of the road.

What was it doing there, I wondered? Where was it going? Suddenly a whole new world had opened up to me. In fact, I'd already seen part of the Broads years earlier as a boy, although it hadn't really registered. My grandparents were in the licensed trade, and they did a couple of holiday management stints at Horning Ferry, the pub next to the point where the chain ferry crossed the River Bure.

There are many different facets to Broadland scenery. As you gaze at this tranquil setting, the most difficult thing to grasp is that what you're looking at isn't the perfectly natural landscape that it seems. Beautiful lakes fringed with reeds gently swaying in the breeze, an abundance of plants and birdlife, deciduous woodland – it surely couldn't be anything else, could it?

But as you move along the waterways which join these lakes – or Broads – you pick up the odd clues. Here and there the rivers appear unnaturally straight, and if you're really on the ball, you might spot the numerous windmills which dot the countryside and make a connection. Of course, they're not mills at all, but the drainage pumps which have had a lot to do with the shaping of the landscape.

Believe it or not, Broadland – Britain's prime wetland area, brimming with Sites of Special Scientific Interest – is one of the best examples of an industrial landscape softened by centuries of simply letting Nature take its course. Until fairly recently the assumption was that they were left from when the area was under considerably more water. In fact, however, the Broads are the result of around 500 years of massive peat diggings in the Middle Ages, with subsequent flooding by rising sea levels.

Windpump once used for drainage, Halvergate Ma[...]

The surrounding fens, on the other hand, are down to regular intervention – largely the result of constant reed cutting. Norfolk reed has been used for thatching for hundreds of years, and it's still the best natural roofing material you can get, outlasting a wheat-thatched roof by many years. Left to its own devices, the fenland surrounding the Broads would gradually revert to woodland over a period of about 25 years.

For me, what makes the Broads so special is that they're uniquely different from any other of our National Parks. You won't find any lofty peaks here, no waterfalls tumbling down craggy rock faces, no wild and mysterious moorlands. Few parts of Broadland are very far removed from 'civilisation', and yet you can still experience the most wonderful feeling of isolation.

While some of the footpaths are quite good, you need to get out on the water to do it properly. I reckon you can't beat renting a Canadian canoe from one of several places on the Broads, and paddling out among the reeds, away from the places frequented by the trippers in their motor cruisers.

Cockshoot Dyke, formerly ...lluted but now supporting water lilies

I tend to avoid the Broads at the height of summer when holiday visitors cruise up and down the waterways. At either end of the season it is a different story, or even in the winter, when you can see how a glistening frost, a little ice at the water's edge and a pastel sky can really grip the imagination. Somehow the sky seems so much bigger here – it's hard to discount the thought that you might actually have wandered into a watercolour painting.

If you're lucky, you may see one of the few preserved wherries – sailing boats built as cargo carriers in the days when roads were few and the rivers were the main method of transportation. There's no more stirring sight than the Albion with its big black sail, proceeding majestically down the river.

At one time, it seemed the Broads were in danger of being lost forever. The Common Agricultural Policy's twisted economics had encouraged farmers to 'improve' the centuries-old traditional grazing land by draining it and turning it over to arable production. Fertiliser run-off from the fields mixing with the results of poor sewage treatment had resulted in the water clouding over, killing off the plant life. With no natural protection, the river banks were becoming eroded by passing pleasure cruisers.

But the Broads Authority managed to turn the situation around, with exciting projects such as those at Cockshoot Broad and Barton Broad, where the water quality has been returned to a pristine state, with wildlife flourishing. While the pressures on other areas of natural beauty are rather different from those of the Broads, there is one sad and unassailable fact. The Broads won't stay the way they are for ever.

It's becoming generally accepted that as global warming causes sea levels to rise, it will be uneconomic and indeed impracticable to defend all of Norfolk's coastline. The current sea defence strategy allows for holding the line in some places, and allowing a natural encroachment in others. The hope of course is that the strategy will protect the Broads flood plain, but who knows what the future holds?

It may take fifty or a hundred years, but there's a good chance that eventually the sea will encroach into the Broads, perhaps returning the area to something akin to its state in Roman times. Enjoy it while you can.

Typical grazing scene, Halvergate Marshes

John Bainbridge
18 Stillness beyond silence: Aune Head, Dartmoor

At first there is an absolute stillness beyond silence, with not even the sound of water to break the peace as it seeps quietly from the great mire and into the moorland river. Then at last skylarks soar into the blue and a curlew cries as the walker becomes accepted as part of the landscape. This is Aune Head in the heart of Dartmoor, the most southerly stretch of wild country in the British Isles.

In urbanised and overcrowded southern England, it is hard to imagine that there are still such places as this watershed mire – where you can linger for days on end and see nothing but ground-nesting birds, circling buzzards and a scattering of sheep. Walkers are rare, and shepherds come just a few times a year to check on their flocks, the peace broken by their shouts and the barking of their dogs.

This part of the moor is a vast plateau with none of the steep slopes and familiar rocky tors of north or east Dartmoor. Sometimes the only movements that catch the eye are the cloud shadows chasing across miles of moor grass or the bog cotton blowing in the breeze. The quarter of a million residents crowded around Plymouth probably don't realise there is such peace and solitude a dozen miles away; though it is waiting for them at the moment when they realise they need to escape the 21st century.

View over Dartmoor

There is no better Dartmoor tramp on a still spring day than to the moorland fastnesses around the long slopes of Ryder and the birthplace of the River Avon – the name the Aune takes as it tumbles a rocky course away from the great mire. It was on such an ascent of Ryder, the highest summit on southern Dartmoor, that I first discovered Aune Head many years ago.

Climbing the hill is the prelude to reaching the secret world of the mire. Ryder is vast, its shoulders and spurs covering a dozen square miles of Dartmoor. The most satisfying way up is from Combestone Tor, a huddle of rocks situated where the lower heights of Ryder fall dramatically into the gorge which hides the River Dart.

It was near to this line of ascent that twelve knights of King Henry III rode to delineate the bounds of the ancient hunting Forest of Dartmoor from the moorland commons of Devon in 1240. Not a lot has changed in the eight hundred years since. The ground is still as boggy, the moor grass as pale, and the views over much of south Devon just as extensive. Beyond all that is a sense of space that is rare in southern England.

Tramping up Ryder is a bit like being a fly on a gently inclining wall. You feel tiny in the great sweep of the landscape. On harsh winter days, with the cold air blowing from the north, your feet crack down on the frozen surface and un-melted hailstones. There is scant shelter on this slope from the unremitting attentions of a fierce gale, except in the the occasional peat hag or the isolated hollows and banks where medieval tinners scratched for tin. Yet on brighter summer days you can sunbathe on this same hillside, almost feeling that you can reach up and touch the blue of the sky.

Combestone Tor, Dartmoor

Summit of Ryder's Hill, Dartmoor

The summit of the hill is undramatic, and you might scarcely know you are there but for an abandoned triangulation post and two older granite stones marking the boundary of Dartmoor Forest. Beyond the top, two great ridges lead off to the cairn-capped subsidiary hills of Snowdon and Huntingdon, and the valley of the Avon. For miles around all is moorland, the great tors of the Dartmoor central belt and, beyond, the higher summits of the north moor and the great plateau around Cranmere. On sunnier days a patchwork quilt of red and green fields mark the cultivated lands to the south, won out of the wildwood by Saxon settlers who would use this moorland for the summer grazing of their cattle.

A thread of narrow paths leads down from Ryder to Aune Head. Even on summer days these give some indication of how wet the ground is, as boots squelch and sink slightly through the grass and into the peat. Then a wider track, or rather series of roughly parallel pathways, is reached – the Sandy Way, which skirts the head of the mire on its journey from Holne to Princetown.

Two hundred years ago when French and American prisoners of war were incarcerated at Princetown, a market was held just inside the gates so that the captives might buy or barter for food. On market days a colourful procession of local farmers and traders would walk or lead pack ponies along this lonely route to the prison. Now only the occasional rambler follows in their footsteps.

A mile further north, a line of crosses, markers on the bare moor, show an old monastic trail, almost the only man-made objects standing out on the great expanse of heath. Many years ago, waylaid by a mist returning from Aune Head, I discovered their usefulness as handholds through the wilderness, finding the next before the one behind was quite lost from sight. The travellers who took such a route in medieval times would have understood the solitude of traversing wild country in a way that we find difficult to comprehend. Only by being out in the wild for long enough do we cast off the unwelcome comfort of the crowd.

That is why places like Aune Head are not to everyone's taste. One walker I know was overcome with a physical dread at the desolation around, the miles of empty moorland, the great mire itself with its pools of water reflecting a grey sky, the bright and weird green of the sphagnum moss and, above all, the utter silence of a winter's day when even the birds didn't cry.

Dartmoor is like that. You either feel at home in such a place or are overwhelmed and can't wait to get away. The featurelessness of the moor makes navigation difficult, and some walkers have a genuine fear of getting lost. But for those in tune with these wild surroundings, there are rich rewards, complete with peace of mind and a sense of falling out of time – an uncommon feeling on this overcrowded island.

Sometimes we need to get a little bit lost in order to find ourselves. Aune Head, the real heart of the moor, is a good place to start.

Snowdon horses from Plas y Bre

Childe's Tomb, Monk's Way Path

Wales

Tom Hutton

19 Just a perfect day: Snowdon Horseshoe

It would be waxing a little too lyrical to call Snowdon wild. Her flanks have been unscrupulously mined and quarried for millennia; her summit has been desecrated by an unsympathetic concrete café, and every half-hour – from March to October – any remaining trace of solitude is shattered by another trainload of noisy, insensitive tourists. She's even surrendered her true Welsh name, Yr Wyddfa – the burial place – for a less poetic English title that says so little about her.

But she is still the highest mountain in Wales, and it is still possible to enjoy her wild side, even in the middle of summer. It just requires some careful planning – and a good alarm clock. I'll always remember my first time…

I set off before dawn grateful for the warmth of my breakfast, yet still shivering in the early morning chill. An older and wiser me would have stopped to pull on an extra layer or two; but in the prime of my irrational youth, I couldn't afford the delay – being first on the mountain was my only concern.

lydach Ironworks

nowdon horseshoe at dusk

The Pyg Track proved a challenging introduction in the pre-dawn dark, and I tripped and stumbled frequently as I hurried along the rocky, man-made path. A few stubbed toes felt like a small price to pay to for the joys of having Crib Goch all to myself. The rocky nick of Bwlch y Moch marked a welcome end to this laborious and rather unrewarding section, and as I peered out over the valley below, I was pleased to see the pale light of the coming day finally brightening the eastern sky – the scrambling was going to be a lot easier if I could see where I was going.

I caught my breath – confident that no one was right on my heels – and braced myself for the moment I'd been waiting for – my first-ever mountain scramble. Then, with the light improving all the time, I reached out a nervous hand and placed it firmly and purposefully on the cold, grey rock.

The first few moves were as nervous and awkward as I'd expected – I had no idea whether I was up to this. But I soon settled into a comfortable rhythm and made my way effortlessly up to the cramped platform which forms the mountain's eastern summit.

It was a moment of mixed emotion. On the one hand I was elated; I'd ticked off my first scramble with effort to spare. But on the other hand, I was now face to face with Crib Goch's infamous knife-edge arête, in the flesh, for the first time. It was every bit as fearsome as the pictures suggested: a razor-sharp tightrope of jagged rock, slung tightly between the mountain's two slender summits. I suddenly felt very nervous.

*Snowdon horseshoe
from Plas y Brenin*

I needn't have worried. Despite the exposure – the rock falls away steeply on both sides – the narrow ridge was definitely more bark than bite; and what teeth it did bare were more intimidating than savage. With precise and purposeful movements, I edged my way, inch by inch, along the narrow crest. A slip would have meant a lot more than a dusty behind, but I wasn't going to slip; the holds were reassuringly large, and there were plenty of them. The further I went, the more I enjoyed myself; scrambling was something I could definitely get into. I started to wish it would go on forever.

Sadly it didn't, and the western summit came along far too quickly. I celebrated my success with a cup of tea and a homemade flapjack, which barely touched the sides – I'd been so engrossed that I hadn't noticed how hungry I was. The sun had finally made its weary way above the horizon, and Snowdon's dome-like summit now loomed large above me, at the head of the valley. Vandalism or not, she was still an incredibly beautiful mountain, and I was now getting impatient to be standing on her shapely top.

famous Crib Goch
des, Snowdon

uthor on Bwlch y Moch,
n on the day in question

I moved on, clambering comfortably over the Bwlch Goch pinnacles, as if trying to squeeze every last drop of scrambling out of the mountain. Carnedd Ugain provided further entertainment, with some wonderful and unexpected moves along the rarely depicted crest of Crib y Ddysgl. By the time I reached the trig point, I found myself wondering why this 1065 m understudy didn't earn more plaudits.

From there, I dropped easily into Bwlch Glas, where the mountain railway revealed its industrial ugliness for the first time; and I followed its incongruous course steadily upwards towards the boulder-strewn summit. Apprehension took hold again. How would it feel finally to stand on the highest ground in the land? Would I have it all to myself? Would the moment be as special as I had hoped? Or would it be spoiled by the blasphemous developments that had long abused this truly sacred spot?

I was pleasantly surprised. With my back to the intrusive edifice of the café, and engulfed in the silence of the early morning, I found Snowdon, or Yr Wyddfa, as I was now sure she'd rather be called, calm and at peace with her world.

My effort had been rewarded and I enjoyed a few special moments alone with her. I snuck behind a rock to drink my final cup of tea, watching the waters of the Glaslyn glisten hypnotically in the sunlight, like sparkling jewels set in a rugged surround of sinister black stone. Crib Goch looked a little friendlier from this perspective, and I could even make out the odd patch of grass on its southern slopes.

I could also see other people now, although from up here they looked more like ants, and their progress appeared slow and laboured against such a dramatic backdrop. I smiled smugly, knowing I'd be long gone before they reached the top. And I also wondered how much further I'd get before I finally muttered the first obligatory 'Good morning'.

On that note, I shouldered my pack and set off down the South Ridge to start the final leg of my mini mountain odyssey. It had been just the perfect day. And unlike Lou Reed, on this particular occasion I was glad I'd spent it with no one.

Crib Goch pinnacles with Carnedd Ugain and Snowdon in background

Jeremy Moore

20 Wildest Wales: Upper Rheidol, Mid Wales

The Hengwm valley is remote and atmospheric, rarely visited but easily accessible. It is broad and boggy-bottomed, inhabited mainly by sheep – and not many of those – and surrounded by high rounded hills with few distinguishing features. The area is an ocean of green in summer but it comes alive in a visual sense with the rich, earthy colours of autumn and winter. For a slice of 'Wild Wales' it would be hard to beat.

Despite its apparent wildness though, there are traces of human presence throughout the area. It is difficult to believe that it was ever farmed, but the oldest maps show islands of cultivation amongst the rough grazing. There are four ruined houses, in various states of disrepair, in this section of the valley. They are melancholy reminders of harder times and tougher people, and around them one can still almost hear the laughing voices of children. They were gradually abandoned during the first half of the last century, and the process of de-population was completed in 1960 when Nant-y-moch farmhouse, a little downstream, was cleared to make way for the reservoir of the same name.

Hengwm Valley with the Hyddgen entering from right

'Hengwm' is a misnomer, however, because its geomorphology makes it the Upper Rheidol. The very first Ordnance Survey dating from the 1820s shows the Rheidol 'becoming' the Hengwm just above the present reservoir. But estate maps of 1788 show the river's name changing from the Rheidol to the Gelli Gogau, and do not mention Hengwm at all. The coming of the Ordnance Survey must have set the names of natural features in stone, whereas in earlier times they may have been more fluid – in remote areas depending, perhaps, on one man's preference.

To complicate matters further, Llyn Llygad Rheidol (Lake of the Eye of the Rheidol), lying just beneath the north face of Pumlumon Fawr, flows into the Rheidol. The watercourse joining the two is known as Nant-y-Llyn, and is little more than a mountain stream. One wonders whether an early writer with romantic pretensions was responsible for this confusion. Perhaps he was one of the early Pumlumon guides, because the true source of the Rheidol is three miles north-east of the lake as the raven flies, in a bog.

The Hyddgen is a short tributary on the north side of the Rheidol which has a momentous place in Welsh history. In 1401 Owain Glyndwr, here in his Pumlumon stronghold, defeated an English army at the Battle of Hyddgen. Exactly where, however, we do not know. One writer quite confidently proposes a location of the same name uncannily adjacent to the farmhouse, now ruined to the north. A second authority builds up a powerful scenario for a battle on the summit of Carn Hyddgen to the east, while a sword has been found at a third site about a mile to the south, near the confluence of the Hyddgen and the Rheidol.

Two quartz blocks – Cerrig Cyfamod Glyndwr – near the latter site are said to mark the signing of a document by victor and vanquished. Others have pointed out that a battle site would be quite extensive, so perhaps there is some truth in each claim. But perhaps the exact location of the battle is unimportant. What matters is the atmosphere in the valley, which R S Thomas, Welsh poet par excellence, captured perfectly in his poem Hyddgen:

The place, Hyddgen;
The time, the fifth
Century since Glyn Dwr
Was here with his men.
He beat the English.
Does it matter now
In the rain? The English
Don't want to come:
Summer Country.
The Welsh too:
A barren victory
Look at those sheep,
On such small bones
The best mutton,
But not for him,
The hireling shepherd.
History goes on;
On the rock the lichen
Records it: no mention
Of them, of us.

from Tares, © Kunjana Thomas 2001,
reproduced with thanks to Gwydion Thomas

Gatepost, Nant-y-llyn

Hyddgen (left) and Hengwm Valleys at dawn

George Borrow probably walked this way between Machynlleth and Ponterwyd, and it is still possible to make this journey today on foot or mountain bike. Some years ago I was taken aback to see an ancient Rover saloon being driven through the ford on the Hengwm, still quite a formidable river at this point. The driver wound down his window and said he was on his way to Devil's Bridge from Machynlleth and asked if this was the right way?

A short tributary further east known as Cwm Gwerin (earlier the Gwarin) feels, despite its relative proximity to tarmac, as if it could be the most remote place in Wales. The valley rises quite steeply from the Rheidol and swings south before coming up against the bulk of the Pumlumon massif. It is an altogether more rugged affair than its parent, and unusually for this part of Wales, has a number of broken crags on its sides. When they are in occupation, a pair of peregrines will shriek angrily at the visitor, and argue endlessly with their neighbours – a pair of ravens.

Cwm Gwerin is also the home of the writer and zen practitioner Ken Jones, resident of the lower Rheidol, but also part-time hermit of the crags. Now well into his seventies, Ken spends periods of days high in the valley with little but the weather and his thoughts for company. In a concession to his advancing years and weary bones, he now takes a tent. But for many years he sheltered and slept high up on the mountainside, in a cave with a sheep's skull set into the drystone wall he has built. It was likely, he maintains, to have been home to Owain Glyndwr and other saints and outlaws before him. I'd like to think that one day the cave might become known as 'Ogof Ken Jones'.

The Upper Rheidol is not ecologically truly pristine, and is not particularly valuable for its wildlife. But we should value it for its feeling of wilderness alone. Traces of a human past add a further dimension to the landscape, and seem to add to its grandeur.

To the north and west of the river lies Strategic Search Area D, thought by the Welsh Assembly to be suitable for large-scale wind farm developments. How would we feel if every hilltop and ridge were crowned by wind turbines? Would they ruin or destroy the area, as the anti wind farm campaigners believe, or add to the sense of being in a living, breathing and evolving landscape?

Sheep skull

David Bellamy
21 The wrong trousers: Cwm Clydach, Mid Wales

For some strange reason I was wearing a new pair of trousers when I decided to seek out the view of the Devil's Bridge from downstream: I could not wait to sketch it and locate the face of the Devil himself.

The route involved scrambling down a 150-foot bouldery, briery bank and two crossings of the Afon Clydach, although as I set off I had no idea if this would locate the view I sought. By the time I'd made the second crossing, with water up to my knees, my trousers were new no longer – in fact they were an abject mess.

River Clydach below Devil's Bridge

Much tree detritus had been swept downriver, and I balanced unsteadily on this to sketch, the pencil stabbing in unseen features with each lurch. At this point the gorge narrows between vertical cliffs, with a plunging waterfall of immense power directly beneath the Devil's Bridge. Little sight of the bridge filtered through the trees, but etched into the right-hand cliff only a few feet away hung the grim features of Old Nick, his nose dripping with moisture pouring down the rock.

From that moment I became hooked on the Clydach Gorge, a huge rent in the escarpment west of Abergavenny, on the far eastern edge of the Brecon Beacons National Park. Here the river, wild and uninhibited in places, cuts through a capping of millstone grit into dramatic carboniferous limestone, and finally reaches old red sandstone as it tumbles some 700 feet down a rocky staircase before winding gently through meadows to join the Usk.

It boasts a surprising number of spectacular waterfalls hemmed in by ivy-hung cliffs, and even a natural rock bridge. Cottages cling to the steep sides, seeming to defy gravity. Because of this steepness, the Ordnance Survey map is greatly challenged to depict so many features stuck on top of each other. Many paths are overgrown, yet yield hidden secrets, even close to the busy A465 along which thunders heavy traffic. In summer this lies mainly hidden from those walking the paths, with the noise thankfully muted by the beech canopy.

Whatever the season, for the artist and photographer, the plunging precipices and wild torrents present formidable compositions which arouse a strong sense of self-preservation in the eye of the beholder. 'The very soul of Salvator Rosa would hover over these regions of confusion' as painter Edward Dayes commented in the 18th century when acknowledging the subliminally-wild subject tastes of the Italian Master. He could easily have been referring to the Clydach Gorge.

Straw stalactites in Ogof Craig a Ffynnon

Clydach Ironwo

One of my favourite tactics is to work my way up the river bed, sketching from a rocky ledge, or perhaps while standing in the river. The enforced discomfort invariably acts as a spur to reduce over-working, but amid such glorious savagery, the discomfort is hardly noticeable.

I often feel the gorge is at its best in truly wet weather, when the Clydach becomes a roaring mass of water, forced between restricting limestone walls. The cliffs come alive as water gushes out of cracks, crevices and caves, for the gorge is riddled with a maze of intricate cave systems.

Not far upstream from the Devil's Bridge lies a sinister black hole in the bed of the river about 60 feet deep, a fitting lair for the most foul of monsters. This is a resurgence from the labyrinth of underground passages beneath Llangattock Mountain to the north. At times divers descend into the murky depths to clear a way through, for the exploration of these hidden caves continues. Clearing the bottom of the pool is a never-ending task, as boulders are constantly forced back by the action of floods.

Up a tributary on the south side just below Old Nick's iron gaze, you will find Shakespeare's Cave, the entrance guarded by savage rock fangs under which a small stream emerges, looking for all the world like the very Gateway to Hell. Clad in wellies, you can duck under the fangs and then walk a short distance into the cave before it becomes a tight rift, followed further along by passage so low that in places it can only be negotiated under water. Being rather too big and awkward for restricted passages, I found it a challenge towards the far end simply to turn round for the exit journey.

William Shakespeare is said to have visited the gorge and been inspired to write *A Midsummer Night's Dream*. It is difficult to imagine a finer setting for the play than Cwm Pwcca ('the bogey's dingle') in the heart of the gorge. By day, Cwm Pwcca is a place of tranquil beauty, but at night to those with imaginative minds it can be transformed into a place of horror. It is said that the Devil would appear at the side of the unsuspecting wayfarer in the guise of a large black dog, only to disappear in a ball of fire.

Down the centuries the gorge has been abused like few other areas. As early as the 17th century, iron-making was carried out, and expanded later with the building of the Clydach Iron Works. The ruins, weathered and crumbling, still stand in the lower gorge, a monument to the toil and sacrifice of the workers. The life of the iron-workers was vividly brought to life in Alexander Cordell's *Rape of the Fair Country*.

Tramways and inclines connected the various levels and in the mid 19th century, a railway was laid through the southern side of the gorge, with tunnels to accommodate the line. Long closed, it must have been a spectacular ride up to Brynmawr at the head of the valley. The minor road eventually became developed into what is now the A465 Heads of Valleys Road. Even the abandoned quarries have now mellowed into the landscape.

The great blast furnaces no longer roar, and the steam hammers, rolling mills and coke yards have fallen silent. Yet the gorge is once again under threat from the proposal to widen the main road into a dual-carriageway, even though the existing road is still below capacity.

Yet another glorious slice of wildscape, not just within a National Park but including a Site of Special Scientific Interest and a National Nature Reserve, will be sacrificed to the road lobby. But Cwm Clydach has repeatedly cast aside the efforts of man to reduce it to rubble, remaining defiant against all those who seek to exploit it.

It is still one of the most dramatic, historically fascinating and visually exciting parts of the Brecon Beacons National Park – and well worth sacrificing several pairs of trousers in the cause of a day's exploration.

Icicles in Clydach Gorge

Alf Alderson

22 A bit of a slap: Whitesands Bay, Pembrokeshire

Every now and again I'll go surfing at a local beach and something – maybe the tang of salt spray from the breaking waves or the wail of a gull swooping overhead – will transport me back to my first surf sessions in Pembrokeshire 25 years ago. And that brief trip back in time is enough to remind me that much of what was best about that period still lingers indefinably in the air today.

It was a time when we left familiar Pembrokeshire waves behind and went off either with friends or alone on 'surfari' to discover the waves and cultures of Europe's Atlantic coasts, Sri Lanka, Indonesia, Australia and the South Pacific.

Lone surfer, north Pembrokeshire

Surfer 'in the barrel'

But more than this, it was a time when friendships were developed back in Pembrokeshire based almost exclusively on this obsession with surfing; friendships which in most cases drew us back here from all those more exotic corners of the globe. It certainly can't have been the local surf that was the big attraction! Indeed, the ironic thing about these relationships is that they're grounded as much in the hard times as the good times.

Those long, warm summer days and user-friendly swells that we all live for often attain a golden glow that can easily blind you from the reality: that on the best-known beaches, you're invariably competing with huge numbers of visiting surfers to ride small, unthrilling summer surf. Each session is so similar to the last that it tends to blend one into the other, and become little more than a blur of fuzzy memories from which you can't isolate separate incidents – who did or surfed what, when they did it, where they did it or why.

On the other hand, days such as February 18, 1989, stand out in the minds of half a dozen people with whom I still surf. We were the only ones riding the waves that mid-winter day, when all the wannabes were tucked away in their warm city offices day-dreaming about the coming summer's surf. And what we were riding was one of the cleanest and biggest surfable groundswells to hit Pembrokeshire in a long time.

My mate Tony Kitchell, who now spends winters surfing the big swells of Madeira, and with whom I've surfed and drunk to excess all over Europe on and off since 1980, claimed that the waves at Abereiddi were breaking at 15 feet (4.5m) that day.

Whitesands Bay, calmer weat

That's big for Pembrokeshire, and anywhere else for that matter. My local break (surfing spot) Whitesands was easily double overhead (a surfing term which compares the wave face to the height of a 6-foot person, i.e. it was about 12 feet high). I didn't really have time to register the size of the swell as I rolled up to the beach with an hour of daylight left, scrabbled into my wetsuit and sprinted down the shoreline to paddle out.

I did briefly notice that there were only about six people in the water and the lines of swell stretched far out into the bay, and I also clocked Tony paddling back out just behind me after having caught a wave. A big set lurched shorewards as we were making our way out to sea. I just scraped over it, but it landed right on top of Tony and snapped his board in two, ending his session for the day.

Meanwhile, the few other surfers who'd been out in the water had either ridden a wave in or been washed ashore by that same set, so when, after a long, hard paddle I made it out beyond the breaking waves, I found myself alone. And I found I finally had time to assess the situation properly, something I really ought to have done before paddling out. What I saw were huge thick wedges of water marching shorewards before exploding as heavy, thick waves with a resounding 'whoomp!' to leave behind a hiss of foaming ocean and the boil of sandy water uprooted from the sea floor.

Back on shore I could see Welsh team surfer Chris Payne walking down the beach, board tucked under his arm, and Tony standing in the car park with the two halves of his board beside local surf shop owner Nick Sime, with whom I'd done my first surfari to Portugal nine years earlier. All were wetsuit-clad, but clearly finished with surfing for today.

The only way I was going to get back among their number was to catch a wave in, and soon, as it was getting dark. I experienced both thrill and fear when I eventually committed to taking off on my wave of choice, accelerating down the face before being buried beneath a small avalanche of water as the whole wave broke along the entire length of the beach.

I was underwater for a long time, eventually surfacing to grab my board, take a look out at more walls of water racing towards me and realise that it would be a huge mission to paddle out through that lot again and try for a better wave.

So, with just one wave surfed, I rode the white water into the beach. When I wandered back into the car park in the rapidly-gathering gloom I was greeted by laughter and praise for a good 'wipeout'. I think the small group gathered there knew that we'd remember this swell for years to come – even those of us who'd only had the chance to catch one wave of it.

And so we do, just as much as perfect morning sessions in Costa Rica, impeccable swells in the Maldives or busy summer sessions in Pembrokeshire when you get lost out in the surf among people you've never seen before. It's these incidents, with just a few friends being given a bit of a slap by Pembrokeshire's winter waves which makes surfing in this corner of the world memorable, and worth staying for.

I know other surfers who live in even colder corners of the globe – Scotland, Nova Scotia, Norway – who would agree. The waves don't have to be the best in the world, nor does the climate – if the people, the landscape and the spirit of the place are right, that's pretty much all you need.

Abandoned village una Slievemore, Achill Isla

The moment before 'a good wipeout'

Ireland

Christopher Somerville
23 Songs in stones: County Mayo

Olcan Masterson played Old as the Hills on his black whistle when we had finished dancing on the misty top of The Reek – finer music than the heavy breathing, the stumble of boots and the drip of sweat among the stones which had accompanied our little jig of delight.

Not that there was anything particular to crow about. Reaching this modest summit is something that hundreds of thousands do each year. But there is always magic in the moment when you come up over the edge after the long stony slog and stand panting against the chapel wall. A chink opens in the eternal cloud of The Reek to spread fifty miles of mountains, islands and wild sea coasts before you like a feast. Even if you never dance, never sing, now you do.

On Garland Sunday, sixty thousand ascend the rubbly cone of The Reek, County Mayo's holy mountain of Croagh Patrick. And did the feet of St Patrick in ancient time walk upon this bare mountain top? Reek pilgrims believe so – some of them. Some climb barefoot, counting each bruise a blessing.

re Island and
w Bay

w Bay and
agh Patrick

We had walked in along the pilgrim path from Ballintober Abbey past standing stones and holy wells where Olcan pushed coppers among the chinks of the stones and left strips of his handkerchief knotted in the elders and hawthorns of the wells. Pagan airs and earthy tunes of praise trailed behind him.

Not all traditional musicians feed off their landscapes, even among perspectives as wide as those in the west of Ireland. Some keep brooding in the dark bars of the towns, developing a competitive and panicky edge to their tunes. But music and landscape have a way of intermingling in Mayo, and when you are walking with a musician as alive and expressive as Olcan you find your own eyes opening too.

The field of Lankhill lies beside the pilgrim path from Ballintober, and Olcan unpeeled the stones from its green skin for me in ways I would never have discovered. He showed me a broken standing stone jagged into the earth in the shape of a lightning streak, and the Mass Rock whose stones concealed the missing piece of the monolith; the stones of a hermit's cell entwined by an ancient blackthorn; nameless stones seeded inside an Iron Age ring fort which marked the site of a 'killeen', a graveyard for unbaptised children; a smooth white curestone of quartz tucked into a hidden chamber at the back of a holy well. Old and new faiths intertwined in a manner that seems entirely natural in the bleakly beautiful landscapes of Mayo.

Mountains and coasts go to make up the essence of Mayo – mountains thick with bog and generally shawled in mist, coasts of black cliffs and changeable seas scattered with islands. Clew Bay, a great bite taken out of the county's seaward flank, holds hundreds of drumlin islands which put me in mind of a host of little green-backed sea monsters all swimming west, baring teeth of yellow clay at the Atlantic.

Keem Strand, Achill Island

Clogh Phádrig standing stone, Lankill

The cliffs of Croagh, Achill Is

Out there on Island More, Didi and Anne tend their organic garden and fight the winter weather in their oyster trawler and jollyboat. I don't think I will ever have another meal as good as the pile of Clew Bay oysters baked in their shells that I ate at the kitchen table on Island More with a pint of Didi's home-brewed beer and a heap of floury potatoes salted with sea wind. That was late on a windy Mayo night, with artichoke spikes tapping at the window and the shadow of a sea otter slipping across the pebbles on the shore beyond.

The wilder the place, the simpler the pleasures. Standing on the empty kelp-strewn sands of Cross Strand on the Mullet peninsula, gazing out over stormy green seas to Inisglora where the Children of Lir flew in the guise of swans, I came as near to unfolding wings and leaving earth as I ever have.

That wonderful music is the thread that binds it all together for me. The town of Westport holds more music than it knows what to do with, and master whistle-player Olcan is the hub round which the sessions revolve in Hoban's or McHale's. Under Olcan's wing I have learned to throw my own portion – some more or less clumsy harmonica playing, one or two Irish songs – into the pot labelled 'great crack'.

Communal playing is a powerful vehicle. When you get that rare musicians' moment in the full blast of a mighty session, the ramp up which you rush all together into lift-off, it's a beautiful thing. But there are other moments, of equal intensity but subtler shading, almost always experienced far from the town.

If joy in living is one strand of Irish music, melancholy is its bitter-sweet counterpart. Nowhere more so than on the western fringes of Mayo, a tragic landscape open like a book for interpretation. Among the corduroy ridges of abandoned potato drills and the grey stone heaps of tumbledown houses you can read the history of desperately hard lives, of poverty and famine, of neglect and emigration.

I first came across one of these famine villages in Scardaun Valley at the heart of the Nephin Beg mountains, five miles from any road or house, where the traces of tracks, field walls and animal pens lay outlined in the blanket bog of the valley bottom like the negative of a photograph that might never have been printed.

It was a tune that Olcan Masterson played among the deserted houses of Toir Reabhach on mountainous Achill Island that had me in pieces. Perhaps it had to do with the unearthly beauty of the stormy morning, with showers racing in from a restlessly stirring sea to brush the purple and black hills into milky grey before hissing on inland, leaving dazzling rainbow segments in their wake. The strength and simplicity of the dozens of dwellings under the hump of Slievemore, the domestic intimacy of their stone storage cupboards and hearths, the rushy fields corrugated with ancient potato ridges and the rutted village road paved with white quartzite, all seemed suddenly unbearably poignant.

'Whenever I'm here, it's as if I hear the shouting and laughing of all those vanished village children' Olcan said, more to himself than me. He put the whistle to his lips and sent the lament Donal Óg – 'Young Donald' – floating between the roofless houses and off down the mountainside.

I had the harmonica out and at my lips to shadow him, but let it fall unblown. The quiet whisper of the rushes and far-off fall of the sea were the only accompaniment the black whistle needed among the cold stones.

Porturlin, County Mayo

Mike Harding
24 Connemara on my mind: Connemara

I can walk from my cottage door in Connemara out along bramble-sided lanes and down to the foreshore of Cleggan Bay. If I follow the tideline northwards, I can strike up the hill which forms the northern arm of the bay, rambling through bog and over rock outcrops until I come to the ruins of an old Napoleonic watch tower.

The tower, square-built of semi-dressed stone, first began to fall after a storm which hit west Connemara in the 1970s. Since then, time and the Atlantic weather systems that rule this coast have picked and gnawed away at the work of those English engineers until nothing is left now but a stump and a jumbled mass of stone.

I often think of those army engineers, probably from places like Bolton or Billericay, ordinary English lads who must have wondered what in blazes they were doing here in this colonial outpost on the western edge of their world. They wouldn't have understood the language, the religion or the ways of the local people, and would have felt as foreign here as the tea planters in Ceylon and the District Officers in Uganda.

e Twelve Bens from
ross Ballynahinch Lake

Sea thrift on the beach

Below the hill is a holy well, one of many hundreds that can be found all over Ireland, and a sign, not just of Ireland's Catholic heritage, but also of its pagan roots. For though these wells are often named after saints like Patrick or Brigid, they are far older than that.

Springs and wells were sacred to the Pre-Christian Irish (as they were to the people of the west of mainland Britain, the Welsh and Cornish in particular, and think of the Derbyshire well-dressings). The custom of hanging rags and bandages to the branches of the trees around them goes back to the days when wells were worshipped as a source of life. Some of the wells are dedicated to the Virgin: Tobar Muire is common here (and is how Tobermory on Mull got its name) but my favourite is Tobar n'Galt – 'the well of the mad' – in Sligo. A drink from it was said to cure ills of the mind.

The well under Cleggan Hill has no name; it is simply marked on the map as Holy Well. I come here whenever I climb this hill. The well is hard to find, Catholic Ireland isn't what she used to be, and it is overgrown, occluded by nature seeking to claim back the land. The place has an atmosphere, as all holy wells do. Pure water bubbles out from the bedrock only yards from a cove where the sea endlessly rolls up a shingle beach.

Sunset at Rosses Point, C

I bring small children here; nephews and nieces, and they play in the sea yards from the well, with Inishbofin in the distance and sea thrift and broom twitching in the Atlantic breeze. It is a special place; and in a way it is a symbol of Connemara itself, which is more a state of mind than a place.

Connemara has no defined boundaries; it is not a political state, and has no TD (*Teachta Dala*, Member of the Dail), no MEP (Member of the European Parliament), no offices, no symbols or insignia. You could loosely describe it as starting just north of Oughterard continuing to Killary Harbour. Eastward it holds the Twelve Bens, and ends at the Mayo border. It is in County Galway, yet it is more than the county in which it sits.

It is great walking country. Climb to the summit of Derryclare and look around you and you will see a land that is half land, half water, with lakes and boglands stretching away to the sea. Across the Inagh Valley lie the Maumturks, a line of quartzite summits which mark the furthest west of St Patrick's travels.

The seaward fringes of Connemara – Spiddal and Carna in particular – are Irish- speaking and have produced a rake of great traditional singers, dancers and musicians. If you want to hear Irish music at its best then seek out Marcus and P J Hernon or Johnny Connolly and you will hear what people call 'the pure drop' - no flash Riverdance stuff, but pure *sean nos* (old style) music and dance.

Galway, both county and town, evoke pride and passion of course, but Connemara means much more. It was to Connemara that the many of the Irish were driven by Cromwell when he sent them 'to Hell or Connaught', and it was to Connemara that J M Synge came, that Padraig Pearse came. As many will tell you, this is the real West.

Synge found his voice here, echoing the stories and the voices of a people poor in everything but language and their imagination. Pearse came here to his small cottage to dream his dream of an Ireland free from the coloniser. The British murdered him in Kilmainham Jail after the Easter Rising of 1916, but his dream lived on.

A place of mountains and lakes, sea inlets and holy wells; it is too easy in a way to romanticise Connemara, to present a picture of donkeys carrying creels of turf to thatched cottages, of red-haired children in Aran sweaters. The truth is nothing like that: Ireland has changed more in the last twenty years than in the previous two hundred; the 'Celtic Tiger' has brought new pressures, new anxieties, new greeds.

Ireland is now one of the most expensive countries in Europe; I bought exactly the same basket of groceries in Andalucia and in Connemara – and the Connemara basket cost more than twice as much. The thatched cottages have gone too, and the landscape painted by Paul Henry is now cluttered with bungalows and threatened with other developments from airports to wind farms.

There is an element of gombeenism (usury) here that is doing more to destroy Ireland than the Brits ever did. Yet I suspect that, just as the English tower above my home fell into decay, the works of the destroyers and the corrupt, visionless ones, to whom landscape is nothing but money, will go the same way. In a hundred years time people will look at their ruins and wonder. Underneath it all, the heart and spirit that is Connemara will survive all their towers, all their vanities.

Peat stacks, Connemara

Jacquetta Megarry
25 Beyond Europe's western outpost: Great Blasket

Standing on the Cró, you can see for miles. To the north-east stand the landmarks of the Dingle Peninsula – the Three Sisters and Mount Brandon, with Mount Eagle to the east. Dingle is the most westerly part of mainland Ireland, itself the western outpost of Europe. To the south-east, MacGillicuddy's Reeks rise in their grandeur, with Carrauntoohil, Ireland's highest mountain, crowning the horseshoe. Scattered around are the outlying Blaskets, basking like hump-backed whales on a ruffled blue sea. To the west, the Atlantic Ocean stretches all the way to the shores of America.

The weather is clear, of course: if it were not, you probably wouldn't be here, as motor boats from Dingle or Dunquin leave in summer months only, wind and weather permitting. Even so, you may have to transfer by rigid inflatable tender, depending on the state of the tide. With the benefit of 21st century nautical technology, then, you may land on Great Blasket on certain days of certain months – and, if the weather deteriorates, you may well be benighted there.

he Blasket Islands, from ear Slea Head, Dingle

Arriving at Great Blasket by rigid inflatable tender

From Great B toward Sybil Poi Brandon Mot

The island was inhabited for many centuries, probably since the Iron Age. The islanders were self-sufficient and stoical to a degree that nowadays is unimaginable. They grew subsistence crops o oats and potatoes by back-breaking cultivation of thin soil in marginal fields. They also caught fish chewed raw seaweed, collected seabird eggs, trapped rabbits and clubbed the occasional seal – while coping with the hazards of wild weather and turbulent seas.

The islanders favoured the naomhógs still made and used in Dingle today. These precarious craft – tarred canvas on a wooden frame – were light enough for two men to carry and well-suited to work with lobster-pots. The people's survival depended on co-operation, giving rise to a strong Blasket identity and 'voice' – at once comic and sardonic, philosophical and lyrical, salty and devou

The islanders were prolific and skilful writers, creating three classics of Irish literature published within seven years (1929-1936). None of the three authors had had more than a village school education, and only one, Maurice O'Sullivan, had ever travelled beyond Tralee. But their accounts of life on Great Blasket capture the oral tradition of fireside story-telling and folk-tales with all the freshness of everyday speech. More widely read in their English translations, the books of the 'Blasket Library' provide extraordinary insights into island life.

Even in the 20th century, the islanders had no machinery, let alone electricity; a cashless, co-operative economy; and a patriarchal society with arranged marriages. Separated from the mainland by Blasket Sound, a narrow channel with many wrecks testifying to its treacherous currents, they routinely had to face difficulty and danger – to collect mail, to trade goods, to see a doctor and to attend church.

Long before its terminal decline, the island's population fluctuated. Of 153 islanders who lived there in 1841, only 97 remained ten years later, survivors of the Great Famine. But a period of prosperity followed, with good catches of fish and stable prices. With valuable seafood catches to trade, the islanders prospered and came to regard their former 'luxuries' – tea, flour, sugar, crockery and cutlery – as necessities. 'The hunting of seals ... was abandoned; the spinning-wheel fell into disuse; the cresset of fish-oil was replaced by the paraffin lamp; the girls began buying print frocks ...' as George Thomson chronicled in *Island Home: the Blasket Heritage.*

Great Blasket's population peaked at 160 during the First World War. A 1930 photograph shows a healthy collection of 20 or more pupils outside the school. But the pressures of the 20th century eventually overwhelmed this fragile island community. By the mid-1930s, young people were realising that the island held no future for them, and the trickle of brave or desperate people venturing west to the 'next parish', America, grew to a steady stream. Already, more islanders lived in Springfield, Massachusetts than on Great Blasket itself, and their relatives soon joined them. Inexorably, the average age rose, pupil numbers fell, and the school closed in the early 1940s. As the older islanders died, their houses were closed up and fell into disrepair.

By 1953 only 22 people were left, too few for a viable community. The Irish Land Commission offered to rehouse the few remaining families in purpose-built cottages with arable land at Dunquin. Arrangements were made for the evacuation of people and belongings on November 17, but the Atlantic again asserted its supremacy, and without the islanders' skilful boat-handling the outcome could have been tragic. The people were finally landed, but most of their furniture and all the telephone equipment had to be abandoned.

Start your exploration by walking around the island from the tiny harbour. Climbing steeply through the village, you soon pass the path down to White Strand, where colonies of playful seals bask on the sandy beach. To the constant raucous chatter of seabirds, continue past Doon Fort, the lesser summit of Slievedonagh and various small clocháns. These dry-stone beehive-shaped buildings were originally inhabited by islanders, and later used as outhouses for animals and for drying turf. Sheep graze peacefully, unfazed by vertiginous cliffs, and oblivious to their fate: Blasket lamb is still served as a speciality in mainland restaurants.

Continuing south-west along the island's rocky spine, you reach Sorrowful Cliff, the height from which fishermen's wives watched one dreadful day in the 1830s when the boats below were smashed by a furious sea when a sudden storm took the lives of 14 fishermen. The walk culminates at the Cró (Croaghmore), whose panoramic views belie its modest altitude (292 m/940 feet).

On the return, you begin to realise how hostile this barren, treeless island would be when lashed by Atlantic winter gales. The only shelter anywhere is in the lee of roofless stone buildings. In season, one of the few restored buildings houses a café with overnight accommodation for a few knowledgeable visitors.

Returning to the village with its roofless ruins only underlines the extreme wildness of Great Blasket. Its houses are peopled by the ghosts of a stubborn, unique community. Their names live on through the Blasket Library, as the names of ferry boats and in the memories of the locals.

E M Forster said of O'Sullivan's portrait of life on the island: 'This book is unique ... an account of neolithic civilisation from the inside'. Returning on the ferry to your 21st century lifestyle, you realise that memories of this neolithic community will linger and haunt you.

Whereas John Muir reminded us that for 'tired, nerve-shaken, over-civilised people ... wildness is a necessity', the Blasket Islanders had to wrest their necessities out of uttermost wilderness.

Sheep graze peacefully on the Great Blasket cliff

Biographical notes

Sir Chris Bonington (Foreword) is the best-known mountaineer in Britain, and was knighted for his services to mountaineering in 1996. He has made a number of major ascents throughout the world, but still loves nothing more than to walk and climb in his local Cumbrian hills.

Roly Smith (Introduction and Port na Curaich, Iona) conceived and edited this anthology. He is president of the Outdoor Writers' Guild, having been its chairman between 1990 and 2001. He is an award-winning freelance writer and editor, editorial manager for Halsgrove Publishing and author of over 50 books on the British countryside.

Hamish Brown (St Kilda) is one of Scotland's best-known mountaineering writers. He has written many books on long distance walking and writes regularly for the *Scotsman* and the *Glasgow Herald*. He lives in Burntisland, Fife, and is a regular visitor to St Kilda.

Judy Armstrong (Outer Hebrides) is a writer and photographer, specialising in adventure travel and outdoor pursuits. Born in New Zealand, she now lives on the North York Moors, and includes it with north-west Scotland, the Lake District and north Wales, in her top spots to walk, scramble, sea kayak and mountain bike.

Chris Mitchell (Loch Diubaig, Skye) read zoology and psychology at Hull, and moved to Skye 26 years ago to study midges. He now runs a small guest house in the north-west of the island. He was a Met Office auxiliary weather reporter for 15 years, with specialist knowledge of weather phenomena and lichens.

Chris Townsend (Northern Cairngorms) is a wilderness devotee and loves to head off into the wilds for months on end. He is the author of 15 books on wilderness travel, including the award-winning *Backpacker's Handbook* and *The Munros and Tops*, the story of his long walk over all the 3000-foot summits in Scotland.

Rennie McOwan (Dumyat, Ochils) is a mountaineer, writer, broadcaster and lecturer. In 1996 he was given an honorary doctorate by Stirling University and in 1997 received the OWG's Golden Eagle Award for his access campaigning. His books include a children's adventure novel, *Light on Dumyat*.

Nick Jenkins (Isle of Man) is a freelance landscape and outdoor photographer based in south Wales. His travels have taken him to India, Nepal and Iceland, as well as most of the British National Parks. He tutors in landscape photography for several organisations and shoots stock images for two photo libraries.

Anthony Toole (Whitfield Moor, Northumbria) was born and brought up on the edge of the Lake District. He has walked and climbed extensively throughout the British Isles and elsewhere, see his website **mysite.freeserve.com/anthony_toole.**

Stephen Goodwin (Cross Fell, North Pennines) is the editor of the *Alpine Journal*. He helped to launch *The Independent* in 1986 and was a staff journalist until going freelance in 1999. He still writes for *Independent* titles, and is a three-times winner of the features award in the OWG Awards for Excellence.

Jon Sparks (Dow Crag, Lake District) is an award-winning photographer and writer specialising in landscape and outdoor pursuits, with over a dozen books to his name, including guidebooks for walkers, climbers and cyclists, and the acclaimed *Outdoor Photography*.

Robert Swain (Morecambe Bay) was born near Blackpool, but moved to near Lancaster in 1952. For many years he worked in an office, but longed for the weekends when he could explore the countryside. Taking redundancy in 1992 gave him the freedom to get out and at the same time be working.

Tom Waghorn (Bleaklow, Peak District) is a founder member of the OWG, and a former chief sub-editor of the *Manchester Evening News*, for whom he is still a columnist and feature writer. A member of the Rucksack and Climbers' Clubs, he has climbed widely from Peak gritstone to Ben Nevis, Mont Blanc and the Karakorum.

Chris Craggs (Stanage Edge, Peak District) was born in North Yorkshire in 1950. He moved to Sheffield to train as a teacher and climb on his beloved gritstone in 1970, and he still lives there, on the edge of the Peak District. He has written extensively in the outdoor press, and has authored several rock climbing guidebooks to the UK and Europe.

Andrew McCloy (Arbor Low, Peak District) lives at Youlgrave in Derbyshire, where he writes books about his twin passions: walking and pubs. He is chairman of the Peak District Local Access Forum.

John Cleare (Hambledon and Hod Hills, Dorset) has been a professional photographer for over 40 years, and has climbed, skied and trekked among mountains and wild places the world over. He operates Mountain Camera, an internationally-known picture source: **www.mountaincamera.com**

Kev Reynolds (Ashdown Forest, Sussex) lives on the Greensand Ridge in Kent, with a view of Ashdown Forest. A respected freelance author, photojournalist and lecturer, he has written more than 40 books, many on his specialist areas of the Alps and the Himalaya.

Clive Tully (Norfolk and Suffolk Broads) is an award-winning outdoor and travel journalist, photographer and broadcaster who has written several guidebooks to the Broads and East Anglia. He has been equipment editor of four walking magazines, and correspondent for many more. His travel features have appeared in most national newspapers.

John Bainbridge (Aune Head, Dartmoor) has walked Dartmoor for over thirty years, and spent nine years as the chief executive of the Dartmoor Preservation Association. He writes and broadcasts on the history, topography and environment of the British Isles.

Tom Hutton (Snowdon Horseshoe) is an award-winning writer and photographer, with an almost insatiable appetite for adventure, and a passion for nature. His work appears regularly in many popular publications, and he has written and illustrated several books.

Jeremy Moore (Upper Rheidol, Mid Wales) is based in mid-Wales. His third book of photographs, *Heart of the Country,* featuring the late William Condry's *Guardian* Country Diaries, was published in 2003: see **www.wild-wales.com**.

David Bellamy (Cwm Clydach, Mid Wales) specialises in painting mountain and wild coastal scenes and has written 11 books, illustrated with his paintings, including *Painting Wild Landscapes*, due to be published in autumn 2005.

Alf Alderson (Whitesands Bay, Pembrokeshire) is an award-winning adventure sports and travel writer based in Pembrokeshire. His work appears regularly in UK newspapers and magazines, and he is also the author of several books on outdoor subjects.

Christopher Somerville (County Mayo) is one of Britain's most prolific travel writers, with 25 books and hundreds of newspaper and magazine articles to his name. He contributes regularly to the *Times, Daily Telegraph* and *Sunday Times*. He also writes and presents radio and TV programmes, and is a published poet.

Mike Harding (Connemara) had an early career with spells as a dustman, bus conductor and boiler scaler before taking a degree in education and later becoming a folk singer and entertainer. Mike is a keen walker and an award-winning outdoor writer and photographer.

Jacquetta Megarry (Great Blasket) is a walker and photographer turned publisher. By 2005, her Rucksack Readers imprint had published 12 guidebooks for long-distance walkers and she had launched a new series *Rucksack Pocket Summits* for climbers of the seven continental summits: see **www.rucsacs.com**.

Acknowledgements

The editor and publisher warmly thank the following OWG members who provided additional photography: **John Cleare** www.mountaincamera.com; **Paddy Dillon** www.outdoorwriter.freeserve.co.uk; **Karen Frenkel** www.karenfrenkel.info; **Jeremy Moore** www.wild-wales.com; **Jon Sparks** www.jon-sparks.co.uk; **Gareth McCormack** www.garethmccormack.com; **Jerry Rawson** jerryrawson@aol.com.

Photographic credits

Jon Sparks front cover, 8, 10, 16, 17, 18, 19, 33, 45, 55, 56, 56/7, 57, 58, 59, 61; Chris Townsend end-papers, 29, 30, 31, 32; Jeremy Moore title page, 11, 97, 98/9, 99, 100; Jacquetta Megarry 13, 38, 39, 119, 120, 121, 123; Hamish Brown 6, 20; Judy Armstrong 15, 21, 22, 23, 24; Chris Mitchell 25, 26 (both), 27, 28; John Cleare 34, 35, 36, 75, 76, 76/7, 77, 78; Rennie McOwan 37, 40; Nick Jenkins 14, 41, 42, 43, 44; Stephen Goodwin 46, 51, 53; Anthony Toole 47, 48, 48/9, 49, 50; Paddy Dillon 52, 54, 110, 112 (lower); Robert Swain 60; David Bellamy 62, 92/103, 101, 102, 104; Jerry Rawson 63, 64 (both), 65, 66, 67, 74, back cover; Chris Craggs 68, 68/9, 69, 70; Karen Frenkel 71, 72; Roly Smith 72/3; Kev Reynolds 10/11, 79, 80, 81, 82; Clive Tully 83, 84, 84/5, 85, 86; John Bainbridge 87, 88, 88/9, 90; Tom Hutton 91/94/95, 93, 94, 95, 96; Alf Alderson 105, 106 (both), 107, 108; Gareth McCormack 109, 111, 112 (upper), 113, 114, 128; Mike Harding 115, 116, 117, 118.

Outdoor Writers' Guild
Words and pictures from the outdoors

The Outdoor Writers' Guild was formed in 1980 and by 2005 had about 200 members, all professionally involved in outdoor journalism, photography or illustration.

Membership is not restricted to writers, but includes other outstanding professional media practitioners in the outdoors, including broadcasters, photographers, film-makers, editors, publishers and illustrators. It is the only group of media professionals whose members are exclusively involved in the outdoor world.

Membership of the Outdoor Writers' Guild is open to all those who are actively and professionally involved in outdoor journalism and photography. It is not restricted to people living in the UK. Most of the best-known media professionals currently working in the outdoor world are members of the Guild, and all are expert and knowledgeable within their particular fields.

 For more information on the Outdoor Writers' Guild, contact the secretary by email: **secretary@owg.org.uk**, or visit the Guild's website at **www.owg.org.uk**.

Rucksack Readers
Adventurous walks worldwide

Rucksack Readers publishes robust, rucksack-friendly books with built-in maps for walkers and climbers, on waterproof paper. The main series is for long-distance walkers, with (by 2005) eight titles covering Scotland and Ireland and four worldwide:

Scotland:
Cateran Trail, Great Glen Way, Rob Roy Way, Speyside Way, West Highland Way

Ireland:
Dingle Way, Kerry Way, Wicklow Way

Worldwide:
Explore the Great Wall
Explore Mount Kilimanjaro
Explore the Inca Trail
Explore the Tour of Mont Blanc

New for 2005, the Rucksack Pocket Summits series is for climbers of the 'seven summits' with *Aconcagua: Summit of South America* the first to be released. For more information, visit **www.rucsacs.com** or phone +44/0 1786 824 696.

ISBN 1-898481-24-5   ISBN 1-898481-19-9   ISBN 1-898481-22-9

ISBN 1-898481-51-2   ISBN 1-898481-20-2   ISBN 1-898481-17-2

 Rucksack Readers, Landrick Lodge, Dunblane, FK15 0HY, UK. email: **info@rucsacs.com**

'Wildness so godful, cosmic, primeval, bestows
a new sense of earth's beauty and size.'
John Muir (1838-1914)